REFUGEES IN AMERICA

MAY 31, 2022
To the wonderful Ann on the Creek Tracy,
what a great stay in your
beautiful refuge!! Your place is
so welcoming and filled with
graciousness! with you to both
Lee Bycel

REFUGEES IN AMERICA

Stories of Courage, Resilience, and
Hope in Their Own Words

Lee T. Bycel

Photos by Dona Kopol Bonick
Foreword by Ishmael Beah

RUTGERS UNIVERSITY PRESS
NEW BRUNSWICK, CAMDEN, AND NEWARK,
NEW JERSEY, AND LONDON

Library of Congress Cataloging-in-Publication Data

Names: Bycel, Lee T., author.
Title: Refugees in America : stories of courage, resilience, and hope in their own
    words / Lee T. Bycel.
Description: New Brunswick, N.J. : Rutgers University Press, [2019] | Includes
    bibliographical references and index.
Identifiers: LCCN 2018058704 | ISBN 9781978806214 (cloth : alk. paper)
Subjects: LCSH: Refugees—United States.
Classification: LCC HV640.4.U54 B93 2019 | DDC 305.9/069140973—dc23
LC record available at https://lccn.loc.gov/2018058704

A British Cataloging-in-Publication record for this book is available from the
British Library.

♾ The paper used in this publication meets the requirements of the American
National Standard for Information Sciences—Permanence of Paper for Printed
Library Materials, ANSI Z39.48-1992.

www.rutgersuniversitypress.org

Manufactured in the United States of America

DEDICATION

Refugees are mothers, fathers, sisters, brothers, children, with the same hopes and ambitions as us—except that a twist of fate has bound their lives to a global refugee crisis on an unprecedented scale.

—Khaled Hosseini

This book is dedicated to all those who have traveled hundreds, often thousands of miles in search of a haven and refuge from horrific conditions in the countries of their birth, leaving family, work, and homes behind. They are human beings who have experienced the worst of the human condition. Their spirit, courage, and resilience reflect the greatness of the human spirit.

The eleven stories in this book provide a lens into what millions around the globe are experiencing today. I remain steadfast in my belief that if we can transcend the limits of political discussion and see refugees as human beings with needs and dreams just like our own, then we can find sustainable, just, and compassionate solutions for them to live lives that are safe, that meet their basic needs, and that are rich with the opportunity to have their deepest hopes and dreams fulfilled.

My hope is that this book will move readers to not only care deeply about the plight of refugees and their resettlement but also deepen their resolve to help.

Profits from the sale of this book will be donated to two organizations that are doing excellent refugee resettlement work and offer many opportunities to support refugees:

HIAS (founded as the Hebrew Immigrant Aid Society) hias.org
International Rescue Committee (IRC) rescue.org

CONTENTS

FOREWORD

I have walked that long road to freedom. I have tried not to falter; I have made missteps along the way. But I have discovered the secret that after climbing a great hill, one only finds that there are many more hills to climb. I have taken a moment here to rest, to steal a view of the glorious vista that surrounds me, to look back on the distance I have come. But I can only rest for a moment, for with freedom comes responsibilities, and I dare not linger, for my long walk is not ended.

—Nelson Mandela

There is no better way to introduce this remarkable book than to begin with these wise words of Nelson Mandela. The human beings you will meet in these pages have endured horrors unimaginable, and yet time and again they stood up and continued their walk toward freedom, toward peace and restoring what has been shattered of their humanity. If only we can see them not merely as refugees but as people who have so much to offer us, who will teach us what it means to appreciate being human, to embrace and be thankful for life.

Often when the stories of those seeking refuge, refugees, reach us, they are pervaded with fear that prevents us from being fully immersed in the human context of such stories. The labels and sound bites of the media do no justice to remind us that no one leaves their home, their culture, their heritage, their customs, their lives for the unknown, to live with uncertainty, to suffer, simply to come to America. People leave their homes, their lands, and their countries behind because they can no longer find life there—life as in the possibility to exist, to be alive. They drag their wounded, but not broken, spirits, looking to start over again, often anywhere, really. How can anyone fear such people?

Lee Bycel has crafted for us a rare gift through the stories of eleven individuals, refugees, who now call America home. He brings his compassion, insight, experience, and deep respect to the interviews with the refugees, offering them the opportunity to speak for themselves. Through this gift of stories about what it means to be human regardless of circumstance, the reader will journey through Eritrea, Guatemala, Iraq, South Sudan, Poland, Syria, Cambodia, El Salvador, Vietnam, Democratic Republic of Congo, and Afghanistan. It is indeed an incredible journey that will change your understanding of the word "refugee" and bring you to meet the human beings behind the labels that often create unnecessary apprehension because of the missing context, the voices of these individuals.

This book is needed now more than ever to reawaken our natural impulses of empathy that are dulled due to the overwhelming rhetoric of threat from the others, who are mothers like us, fathers like us, sons and daughters like us, children like us. If you have ever yearned for love, for acceptance and recognition for simply being human, if you've ever felt loss or pain and hoped for a better life, then you will find in these stories these same yearnings, these same expressions of what it means to be human. Do read with an open heart and witness the strength of the human spirit.

Ishmael Beah, international and *New York Times* best-selling
author of *A Long Way Gone: Memoirs of a Boy Soldier* and
Radiance of Tomorrow, a Novel

REFUGEES IN AMERICA

INTRODUCTION

Are all humans human? Or are some more human than others?
—Roméo Antonius Dallaire, saved 30,000
lives during the Rwandan genocide

My Journey

It is the fall of 2004 and I am traveling through the sub-Saharan desert of Chad, one of the poorest countries on this planet. I have just spent two weeks visiting with Darfuri refugees in several refugee camps. It is extremely hot, and I have been riding in a jeep through the middle of the desert for several hours. There are no roads. All you see is sand. You start to feel a sense of vertigo, losing perspective on where you are, where you have come from, and where you are going. It is unimaginable how our driver knows where to go, but his instincts and his knowledge of the desert guide him in the right direction. I am in kind of a trance, tired, thinking about this commitment I have made to meet some of the dispossessed people from Darfur who have come to Chad seeking safety.

In my reverie, I reflect on how it was that here in the twenty-first century, with all our technological, medical, and scientific advances, it seems that we have not come very far humanly, as here genocide is taking place. Decent, good people who have lived in Darfur for a very long time have

1

seen their lives torn asunder—men murdered, women raped, children stolen into slavery—and their villages and homes burned to the ground. And then, as I gaze out into the desert, I think I see a boy walk out from a wadi, a dry river bed, holding a tin cup and extending it out. We are moving at a very rapid pace, even though the desert is filled with deep crevices and the ride shakes you to your core and you lose a sense of what is real and what is imagined. But as we pass, I see that indeed it is a boy, a young boy, maybe ten years old, dressed in rags. I want to ask the driver to stop. Yet all I do is look as we speed by.

I will never forget that moment. That boy haunts me . . . actually, it is my conscience that haunts me. Why did I not insist we stop? Why did I not give the boy a bottle of water, hold his hand, offer some hope? Let him know that the world does care. That I care for this anonymous refugee boy out looking for firewood to take back to his camp. Who knows what potential that boy has? Who knows the contributions he will make as a human being to his family, his friends, his community? Who knows whether he might be the person that will discover the cure for cancer? Like any child anywhere, he deserves an opportunity to grow and pursue his dreams.

A Visit to a Refugee Camp

When I learned about the unfolding genocide in Darfur, I wanted to bear witness to what these refugees were experiencing. For me, "bearing witness" means being present where the suffering is taking place, listening, observing, and taking in the dire circumstances human beings are facing. The next step is action: increasing awareness, writing about the situation, being an advocate, and raising funds for desperately needed humanitarian services. Under the auspices of the International Medical Corps, I went to see its humanitarian efforts in three refugee camps in Eastern Chad, where Darfuri refugees were fleeing to Kounongo, Mille, and Amnabak.

I will never forget the camps. Large areas of land in the sub-Saharan desert filled with rows of basic tents from the United Nations High

Commissioner for Refugees (UNHCR). Refugees, mostly women and children as the men were dead or remained fighting in Darfur, receiving weekly food rations and cooking on open fires near their tents. Young boys collecting firewood, because if the women did it, they were in danger of being raped by men from Darfur, rebel groups, or nomads. Silence filling the air as everyone was lost in thought about what his or her fate would be.

Over the years I have returned several times and find it hard to believe that most of the people I originally met are still there. Tens of thousands of children have been born and have grown up in these camps. The camps were originally built to provide short-term protection before resettlement.

I keep close in my heart a Darfuri man named Adam, a teacher in Darfur who knew some English. He served as a translator in the Kounongo camp, and I got to know him well. He is a thoughtful, sensitive, and hopeful man. On the wall by my desk I keep a handwritten note he gave me in 2009: "My dear brother Lee, it is really difficult to see you leaving while I remain here in this refugee camp. But I feel so grateful for your commitment to the people of Darfur. I believe that one day we will go home." I have been haunted by his first line. Though most Darfuri refugees have yet to return home, I left, back to my life in the States.

For me, being able to return to my life here brought with it a new sense of responsibility to not forget Adam and the many other refugees I met. I yearned to bring the personal stories of refugees and what I learned from them to life.

The Voice of the Refugee

This is a book of stories, a lens into the lives of eleven refugees who call America home, as told in their own words. The people included here give voice to their journey and those of millions of other refugees. In this book, they tell their stories starting in their home country and leading up to their life here in the United States.

In 2004 when I made the first of what would be many visits to Darfuri refugee camps, I really began to take in the powerful and complex stories of refugees and what they were experiencing: loss of home, life in a refugee camp, trauma, and the yearning to rebuild their lives. There are many experiences that refugees, all around the world, have in common. Yet, so often we reduce their stories to statistics and stereotype their experiences. Each refugee has his or her own anguished tale to tell.

There is an ongoing challenge of seeing the human qualities in others who are different from us. Stereotyping and generalizing allow us to create a simpler world. However, that world lacks the breadth and depth of real human experience. The challenge is to take note of the humanity of others and to understand that most people yearn for basic necessities: safety, shelter, food, love, and the opportunity to pursue their dreams. The refugee situation is not easy to comprehend, especially with all the political rhetoric and internal challenges facing America. There are different types of refugees, from those seeking asylum to unaccompanied minors and migrants looking to find a way to survive financially. The common thread is that they all need safety while seeking refuge in a country that itself was shaped by immigrants and refugees.

The book does not seek to evoke pity. That is not what refugees desire. What I have heard from the people interviewed for this book, along with many others and in the literature I have read, is that they desire empathy, understanding, and an opportunity to demonstrate their value to society.

Dehumanizing Political Rhetoric

The language used to discuss refugees has become so politicized that it has greatly impacted our ability to see them as human beings. Some call them illegal immigrants, aliens, economic opportunists, even murderers and rapists. Often forgotten in the discussion is that "refugee" is a descriptive term referring to people who have had to flee their homes for fear of persecution. They are human beings in pursuit of security and the chance to rebuild their lives. They are people who never wanted to give up their lives in their home country but were forced to do so.

According to the UNHCR, a refugee is "someone who has been forced to flee his or her country because of persecution, war, or violence. A refugee has a well-founded fear of persecution for reasons of race, religion, nationality, political opinion or membership in a social group." A person must meet these criteria to be classified as a refugee by the U.N. This definition is incredibly important as it forms the basis for the legal codification of refugees in the United States and many other countries and differentiates them from internally displaced persons, who have had to flee their homes yet remain in their countries of origin.

In the past few years the political rhetoric about whether to accept refugees in America has become increasingly heated and controversial. The tension for any country is understandable. How do we balance the desire to welcome and protect other human beings who have fled persecution with the need to control our borders and prevent the entry of those who intend to do us harm? The United States is in dire need of a plan that will be humane and equitable. The statistics have become overwhelming and confusing. As new crises take center stage, others become almost invisible to the American public. In the winter of 2019, the president's announcement of a national emergency and the need to build a wall on the southern border dominated the news. Receding to the background are the migrant families that are still separated, the Rohingya Muslim in Myanmar, who are being forced to flee to Bangladesh, and the plight of the Syrian refugees. The media coverage reflects only our short attention spans.

Refugees have been the lifeblood and not a threat to the United States. No person accepted to the United States as a refugee, Syrian or otherwise, has been implicated in a terrorist attack since the Refugee Act of 1980 set up systematic procedures for accepting refugees into the United States. In terms of everyday crime, the literature and studies on this subject show that refugees commit fewer crimes than native-born Americans. Historically, the United States was shaped and developed by immigrants and refugees from all parts of the world.

The "Mouth of a Shark"

Somali refugee Warsan Shire described what it means to be a refugee: "No one leaves home unless home is the mouth of a shark." Though every refugee has a distinct story, they share the loss of home, native language, and culture, the forfeiture of familiar surroundings and society, separation from family and friends, the wreckage of childhood and innocence, the lack of support systems, and the annihilation of the world they were born into. Hannah Arendt, a refugee from Nazi Germany who fled to the United States, captured the sense of loss that many refugees feel. "We lost our home, which means the familiarity of daily life. We lost our occupation, which means the confidence that we are of some use in this world. We lost our language, which means the naturalness of reactions, the simplicity of gestures, the unaffected expressions of feelings."

Refugees are faced with numerous hardships throughout their journey. It is often taken for granted how difficult it is to flee a country. Imagine that you are forced to flee from your home. You must gather your family and belongings. There is usually little time to plan your escape and say your goodbyes to people you will never see again. Factor in potential roadblocks or checkpoints and avoiding most people, as it is very difficult to distinguish between friend and foe. Now you are running for your life, over mountains, through deserts, across seas, and the only thing that will save you is reaching a refugee camp or crossing the border into another country. The people that successfully make this journey are the lucky ones. Thousands try to escape but never make it.

And the journey does not get any easier once you have escaped from your home country. Refugee and displacement camps bring new hardships. Their conditions are usually impoverished, with limited food, water, and medical services, much less education for the children. Often the only protection from the weather is a canvas or plastic tent. Many people in these camps spend years there hoping they will be granted asylum somewhere else. Unfortunately for many, the dream of asylum is nothing more than a dream. This is partly why so many in Africa and the Middle East would rather take their chances crossing the Mediterranean in a rickety and overcrowded dingy in rough seas to reach Europe than spend their time hoping they will make it out of the camp.

A Turbulent History

The history of refugees is long and tumultuous, going back thousands of years. War, religious persecution, political turmoil, and social ostracism, among other issues, have forced people to seek refuge elsewhere. The first use of the term "refugee" in the modern world was in regard to the religious persecution of the Huguenots (white Protestants) in France in 1685, where an estimated 1 million Huguenots fled the country to avoid persecution.

After World War II, the creation of the United Nations dramatically redefined the way states interacted with each other. This transformation and the proliferation of supranational organizations reshaped international law and the entities that fell under its jurisdiction. The U.N. and the UNHCR have profoundly altered how refugees are dealt with and perceived by governments around the world. Before the advent of those groups, refugees were the sole responsibility of states. Sadly, this duty was often neglected. Today, the UNHCR assists refugees and coordinates with states to help resettle them. It offers protection, shelter, education, and health services to the people under its care. What is more, the UNHCR not only assists refugees but also helps displaced people (people living in their birth country but who have had to flee their homes and villages), as many of them eventually will be classified as refugees, if they leave their home country. Without the U.N. and the UNHCR, thousands of lives would be lost to violence and famine, and millions would be living even harder lives. However, with the increase of refugee and displaced populations, the organizations lack the funding to maintain services for greater needs.

As of the spring of 2019, an estimated 68.5 million people are displaced around the world, including 25.4 million refugees, 40 million internally displaced people, and 3.1 million asylum seekers. (There are probably millions more in all of these categories, but it is nearly impossible for the UNHCR to capture the exact figures with so many people on the move.) Many of these refugees are from Syria, Afghanistan, and South Sudan. Those countries have experienced events that are ubiquitous in terms of causing the displacement of peoples and refugees, such as war, famine, and political instability. However, other elements such as religious, political, or racial persecution, gender, sexual orientation, and economics are also factors. When a ruling power decides to systematically persecute and exterminate another group, genocide may ensue; and historically, genocides have played an integral role in refugee crises. The Holocaust and the Rwandan, Armenian, and Cambodian genocides are examples of targeted campaigns to eliminate groups of people that resulted in refugee crises.

The current crises are often compared to World War II and its tremendous number of displaced people. However, those numbers pale in comparison to today. World War II displaced roughly 40 million people. It is astounding that fewer people were displaced in the bloodiest war humankind has experienced than are displaced today. Unfortunately, this current crisis will not subside unless drastic measures are taken. Continuing instability in many parts of the world, the potential for turmoil, and the environmental degradation of the past one hundred years along with global warming will only increase the number of refugees and displaced people.

America's Ambivalence toward the Refugee

The United States has a long history of accepting refugees and displaced people. Pilgrims, fleeing religious persecution, were arguably the first refugees to arrive. Millions of immigrants, many of whom could be classified as refugees, flocked to the shores of the United States throughout the seventeenth and eighteenth centuries because of political, religious, or social persecution. Similarly, the revolutions of 1848 that rocked Europe resulted in extensive bloodshed and ushered in a new wave of refugees and immigrants. It is estimated that more than 3 million people came to the United States between 1845 and 1855. These refugees from Germany, France, England, Ireland, and elsewhere brought fresh ideas and their respective cultures with them. This influx of immigrants and refugees is what makes the United States so uniquely heterogeneous.

However, these newcomers have not always been received with open arms. For almost the entirety of the United States' history, people have been fearful and suspicious of newcomers. These perceptions have created an interesting dichotomy between a country founded on openness and liberal values and its sense of xenophobia that has shaped much of its darker past. The United States' history of refugees is a bumpy road of conflict and angst regarding these newcomers, followed by a sense of acceptance and assimilation, and then a reversion back to nativism. At first, immigrants and refugees experienced persecution and exclusion but eventually assimilated. These new Americans and their heirs then carried out the same acts of xenophobia against the new wave of immigrants that they had experienced years before. This general sense of ambivalence for embracing refugees has also profoundly influenced the government's policy on setting quotas for refugees.

World War II and the United States' vacillation over accepting German refugees is arguably the most famous example of American hostility toward refugees. According to a 1939 Gallup poll, 67 percent of Americans responded no when asked whether the country should allow 10,000 refugee *children* from Germany to come to America. Another poll in 1946 found that 72 percent of Americans disapproved of a plan to resettle Jewish and European refugees. To put this in perspective, current polls show that approximately 50 percent of Americans are against taking in Syrian refugees, fewer than those who were opposed to taking in Jewish refugees.

Time and again, Americans have vehemently opposed resettling refugees in their country. Sadly, history continues to repeat itself. Millions of Americans remain opposed to allowing refugees from Africa and the Middle East to seek safety and shelter here. There is an ongoing, heated debate about refugees and quotas. It raises the question, Why is there so much hatred toward these people? There is no logical explanation for this xenophobia pervading America, an attitude that goes against everything the country was founded on.

The Long Road to Achieve Refugee Status

In this book, each featured refugee survived trauma in his or her native country, and many confronted the challenges of surviving on their way to America. In their stories you will read about inner strength, courage, perseverance, fear, depression, resilience, and luck. They are men and women ranging in age from twenty-five to ninety-two.

There needs to be a program in place so that once people have crossed an international border and become refugees, they do not have to remain refugees forever. The solution may be a voluntary return home in safety and in dignity, local integration in the country of first asylum, or resettlement to a third country like the United States. Most refugees, however, remain in limbo for many years until any of those choices becomes available. The UNHCR estimates that for 10 percent of refugees, the only viable solution is resettlement, but this solution has generally been available to less than 1 percent of all refugees each year. To be resettled to the United States, for example, people must establish not only that they are in fact refugees with a well-founded fear of persecution in their country of origin, but also that they have a special need that qualifies for resettlement under UNHCR criteria, or that they fit into one of the narrow "humanitarian" categories defined by the U.S. government. On top of that, each applicant must undergo intensive interviews by the U.N., Homeland Security, and U.S. contractor personnel, fingerprinting, and thorough security vetting, as well as health screening and cultural orientation. Many refugees are unable to make it through these steps without getting mired in the process. For those who do make it through, it generally takes eighteen to twenty-four months. Finally, after making it to the United States, all refugees are required to reimburse the U.S. government for the cost of their flights.

If refugees are fortunate enough to be granted asylum or to find refuge in America, new challenges emerge. Integrating into a new country is a difficult task that requires a significant amount of work by both the refugee and his or her new country. Imagine moving to a place where you have limited understanding of the language and no family ties or understanding of this new country's culture. It is hard for refugees to successfully assimilate, especially after everything they have been through, lost, and left behind. Countless refugees will experience mental health problems such as post-traumatic stress disorder, depression, or anxiety.

Many of the refugees interviewed in this book shared with me what it was like to arrive after an exhausting flight (for many, their first flight ever) to a new city where they did not know a soul. Exhausted, disoriented, not knowing what to expect, they felt embraced by representatives of a local social service agency who greeted them at the airport and took them to an apartment with a refrigerator stocked with food. In the subsequent days their case manager helped them navigate the neighborhood, enroll in English class, and get their children settled in school. Living in culture shock, they are taken to get social security numbers and eventually driver's licenses.

The refugees shared with me how thrilled they were to be in America, the disbelief of all that they had survived, and their feelings of inadequacy over not knowing how to navigate the system without help. Adults need to find employment within six months. These jobs are often minimum wage. The government assistance they receive from Medicaid and food stamps as well as the generosity of local nonprofits and religious organizations provides them with the financial and emotional wherewithal to settle in. After being in the United States for one year, and if employed, refugees can apply for Permanent Resident Alien status (commonly known as a Green Card). The path to citizenship takes five years.

American Refugee Resettlement Policy

In the United States, the State Department is responsible for determining those refugees who will be interviewed by the Department of Homeland Security (DHS) for consideration for refugee resettlement. DHS is responsible for deciding whether to admit the refugee, but the Department of State is then responsible for the refugee's initial reception and placement in the United States. The Department of State has long done this work through partnerships with six faith-based and three secular voluntary organizations (formerly known as VOLAGS [Voluntary Agencies] but now known as Resettlement Agencies) that have many local resettlement sites or partner agencies around the country to whom they disburse funds for the purpose of assisting refugees with their first few months in the United States. Under the Refugee Act of 1980, the president makes a "presidential determination" before the beginning of each fiscal year, setting the ceiling for the maximum number of refugees to be resettled. In recent years, U.S. policy on refugees has fluctuated significantly. The refugee ceiling has varied greatly and has ranged from as low as 67,000 to as high as 231,700. The Trump administration, however, attempted to lower the 110,000 refugee ceiling set by President Obama for FY2017 to 50,000, though it was thwarted by court challenges and admitted 53,716 refugees to this country. President Trump, however, then set the ceiling for FY2018 to 45,000, which was the lowest since the enactment of the Refugee Act of 1980. It was lowered again for FY2019 with a ceiling of 30,000. Because of "extreme vetting" practices implemented by the Trump administration (ostensibly to further secure the refugee program from terrorist infiltration), the actual number of refugees admitted in FY2018 was 22,491. This and other restrictive policies have prevented thousands of innocent refugees from entering the United States.

Albert Einstein, the Nobel Prize–winning scientist, is one of America's most well-known refugees. There are many others who have played major roles in science, technology, medicine, the arts, business, sports, and every sector of American life. During the Holocaust, Einstein knew how limited the U.S. quotas were for refugees and worked relentlessly to assist his fellow Jews, intellectuals, and others who desperately needed to flee Nazi persecution and extermination. "I am privileged by the fate to live here in Princeton. . . . In this small university town, the chaotic voice of human strife barely penetrates. I am almost ashamed to be living in such peace while all the rest struggle and suffer." His powerful voice echoes the sentiment of many refugees who have seen their loved ones left behind. Einstein lived his life anchored in the roots of his childhood and shaped in the United States that provided an opportunity for him to flourish.

There are also the millions of refugees and children of refugees who contribute to America each day. They are "regular" people who raise children, work in the service industry, coach Little League teams, and own small businesses, and they are fully integrated into life in the United States. Their stories are featured in this book. Like Einstein, they did not forget the culture from which they emerged but have embraced the values and culture of the United States and make many contributions as active and involved citizens.

The Importance of Their Stories

Refugees possess powerful individual stories. This book focuses on eleven men and women who found refuge in the United States. They had been through nightmarish journeys and were fortunate to survive and make it here. Some have done well, while others still struggle. Many lost most of their family in the horrors they lived through or have family back home and are here alone. Many refugees are not ready to share their stories or find it too painful to revisit the past. However, they all live with a story that informs their lives. Those who are willing to speak help us understand the lives that many refugees are experiencing.

This book has allowed me to walk into their lives and hear their voices, their pain and joy, their sadness and their dreams. All of them had to start a new life. All of them still care about the cultural richness of their native land while embracing the diversity and opportunity in America. Each story impacted me deeply and filled me with questions about the nature of perseverance and the ability to cope with the trauma. As I met with these people, I was mindful of all the refugees in America I would never meet—the people we see every day as we go about our lives, who have given up so much to be here. Our country was built and has been shaped by immigrants and refugees, and its future is anchored in the actions that we take today and how we broaden the fabric of American society so that it includes the voices of all, including the refugee.

As Meron Semedar, a refugee from Eritrea, shared with me, "My hope is that one day I will not be viewed as a refugee but simply as another human being making positive contributions to American society."

CHAPTER 1

MERON SEMEDAR

ERITREA

There is an African proverb that has great meaning for me. "He who
does not know where he came from, does not know where he is going."
I know what Eritrea can be and it has lost that. Wherever I am, I will
work towards building a democratic Eritrea that upholds human
rights for all.

Meron Semedar is one of about 40,000 Eritreans living in the United
States. He has made a life for himself here but is torn apart about the continuing human rights violations taking place in Eritrea.

Eritrea lies on the Red Sea, west of Saudi Arabia and Yemen, in the Horn
of Africa, bordered by Sudan, Ethiopia, and Djibouti. The majority of its
5.6 million residents identify as Christian or Muslim. Eritrea faced tumultuous decades of control by foreign powers that had a significant influence on the country's struggle toward "liberation," its current dictatorship,
and its refugee crisis.

Initially composed of diverse ethnic communities, Eritrea came under
Italian control in the late nineteenth century. During the twentieth century,
Italian troops invaded Ethiopia, which led to the foundation of Italian East
Africa, composed of Eritrea, Somalia, and Ethiopia. However, this tri-
partite did not last, and with Italy's participation in World War II, Italian
East Africa became a target. When Italian forces surrendered in 1943, the
British occupied the area and took over administration of Eritrea.

Eritrea became an autonomous federal province within Ethiopia in
1952. But Muslim and Christian religious tensions escalated. The Muslim
League initiated the campaign for Eritrea's independence, while Ethiopia's
Christian Unionist party helped remove Muslims from government jobs,
put an end to teaching in Arabic, ban all other political parties and trade
unions, and impose Ethiopian law on Eritrea. Emperor Haile Selassie dis-
solved the Eritrean parliament and illegally annexed the country in 1962.
This was the beginning of a thirty-year war, until Eritrean independence
in 1991. In 1993, the United Nations recognized Eritrea as a sovereign

country. Isaias Afwerki, who had been a guerrilla leader, became president and shaped Eritrea's only political party, the People's Front for Democracy and Justice (PFDJ). The PFDJ remains Eritrea's only legally sanctioned political party. Eritrea has never held elections at any level of government. Afwerki serves as president for life. In the first few years of being an independent country, the Eritrean people felt empowered and celebrated their victory. After a few years, Afwerki started placing more restrictions and evolved into a dictator much more brutal than Selassie.

Today the United Nations High Commissioner for Refugees characterizes Eritrea's government as a regime whose "rule by fear" dictates a country that is home to a network of informants. People are subject to arbitrary arrest, many disappear, and everyone lives with the ongoing fear of being tortured or executed. Individuals who run afoul of the authorities are often held in harsh conditions in makeshift prisons. Citizens face restrictions on internal movement and speech, and domestic media are controlled by the state. Forced conscription in the military, which can go for decades, is the reason that many people, like Meron, flee.

This dictatorship has fueled the refugee crisis in Eritrea for decades. In 2015, the U.N. estimated that nearly 5,000 men escape across the country's borders each month, and that 400,000 Eritreans—9 percent of the population—have fled in recent years. Upon crossing into Ethiopia or Sudan, Eritreans must decide whether to continue across the Sahara and the Mediterranean to Europe or remain in limbo in refugee camps. In 2018 Eritrea signed a peace agreement with Ethiopia which some feel might lead to the end of forced conscription in the military.

Although he now considers the United States his home, Meron dreams of an Eritrean democracy freed from the shackles of enslavement. He wants to be a force for change.

My calling is to give voice to those who have no voice. I want to see a world where words like human dignity, human rights, respect, kindness, compassion, and peace are more than just nice words. In my

dreams, I believe that this world can be transformed. That will hap-
pen when we each take on a little more responsibility and act to
empower and uplift.

Meron, a man with an infectious smile and a deep sense of gratitude, speaks to the students in my Holocaust and Genocide class every semester. His presentation is deeply compelling and moving. He provides the context of the nightmare that he left behind in Eritrea, his journey, and his life here in the States. The students are spellbound by his remarks, which strike a deep chord within them. Meron acknowledges that each refugee has had a complicated journey and faces many challenges. So he implores the students not to see him and others like him as refugees but as human beings, just like them, trying to shape a meaningful existence.

Hope Is the Oxygen of My Life

It is not an easy road—but hope is the oxygen of my life. I have hope
in humanity.

When Meron Semedar delivered the commencement speech to thousands
of people at the University of San Francisco in December 2016, he spoke
passionately from the podium about hope. His was tested repeatedly
during his journey to freedom that began thirty years earlier in the small
village of Shekha.

Raised in a Country at War

I grew up among soldiers living in a remote part of Eritrea. It was
during the War of Independence from Ethiopia. My father was off
fighting and my mother raised the family.

In Shekha, life was very difficult for Meron's mother, Roma, because
his father, Yemane, a major in the army, was away fighting against the Ethiopian Derg Regime. She decided to move to the Sahel, the northern part
of Eritrea, farthest from the fighting. Like many other women, she played
a key role in supporting the soldiers and was also trained in using the
Kalashnikov rifle. The journey there took nine months (a trip that under
normal circumstances would take a few days by bus) as they had to travel
on foot and on camels, with soldiers to stay safe. During their travels they
saw many people die from Ethiopian helicopter attacks. The vast area of
the Sahel offered her and her children a safe haven. During the War
of Independence many cities emerged there because of the location. Living in the liberated area of the country, life was good for young people.
But Meron did not meet his father until after independence was gained,
when Meron was six.

We felt secure and safe living there. It was an open and accepting cul-
ture where young people could openly share their views. There was

this hope that we were the future generation. In my country's language,
Keyahti Embeba. *It means "the red roses." It's as if they were saying,*
"You are the bright future of this country. You are what we are giving
to this country."

Once Eritrea became an independent country in 1991, Meron and his
family moved to its second-largest city, Keren. It was the closest city to the
villages where his parents were born. The house, made of mud and with
no electricity or running water, was a great improvement from the tents
he lived in during the War of Independence. However, culturally, it was a
very different environment than that of the Sahel.

It was very hard to adjust. We had been living in a very open-minded
place and then we moved to a very conservative society. But my par-
ents, although not well educated, they knew how education could
transform life. It is them who instilled the love of learning and the
great value of education into my life.

His class at the Semaetat Elementary School had sixty students. Three
students shared a table, three tables to a row. The teachers were extremely
strict.

In the science class, besides the average science studies, they would
check our nails, they would check if you have a tissue for your nose,
they would check your ears, are you clean in there, all sorts of basic
things. You got to have those. If you don't, you would be beaten up.
There was punishment.

There were some books, but not enough. Often Meron and his classmates had to take turns copying a chapter by hand onto paper so that they
could study the material.

Meron's mother worked as a cleaner in a hospital. Though his mother
had raised him on her own, both parents were instrumental in encouraging him to succeed in school. Some years later Roma was diagnosed with

asthma. Because of that, Meron needed to step up and help support the family. So, he got a job in construction, hard labor for a child of fourteen. In 2003 his family learned that his father had died five years before in the 1998–2000 border war between his country Eritrea and Ethiopia. By age seventeen, Meron had spent only a total of thirty days, separated into several short visits, with his dad.

Meron attended elementary, middle, and high school and excelled in most of his studies. Although he had great respect for all his classes, as he grew older and entered high school, he found that math and physics classes particularly resonated with him. Every evening after class, he would go to the library to practice equations and finish his homework.

After high school I wanted to go to the university. But as soon as I finished high school, they closed the university and changed the curriculum.

Before, you would finish high school in grade eleven in your city, and then go to military training. Then after the six months of military training, you would either go to the military or join the university depending on your marks in the national exam. But in my time, the university closed and now we had to finish high school in the military training camp with an additional year—grade twelve. Everybody was okay with going to the military training because we took it as our duty, and our older brothers also went through it, but the different part was that after six months of military training, then you spent another year in high school. This really killed the education, the spirit of education, the value of education. The treatment there was militarized, even after you've done the six-month military training. It made many people fed up, including me. I saw no hope in using my education to reach my dreams or build my country. And that's why I decided to leave.

I was eighteen. Many people lost faith in the government and in the educational system even before this whole education and curriculum

change. We had war between 1998 and 2000 against Ethiopia, on a
border issue. That brought the beginning of dictatorship. They impris-
oned many they considered menaces. Then they shut down all private
media. They imprisoned nearly twenty journalists. So, 2001 marked
the start of dictatorship. Everything went hand in hand.

All this was starting to make people fed up. They even punished the
Asmara University students. They took them to the hottest place in
the country, often near 120 Fahrenheit, because they protested against
the government. We all thought that the government didn't care about
educated people, and if you wanted to do something about it, it was
hard, because you were risking your life. So, people started to leave
the country.

Life in the Military

Before we went to this military training camp, they had a program
called "Before It Gets Out of Hand." They used to show on national
TV people who were caught trying to flee from Eritrea to Sudan, from
Sudan to Libya, from Libya to Italy. Libya then was ruled by Muam-
mar Gaddafi, who was a good friend of our president Isaias Afwerki,
so he would catch them, put them in a helicopter and send them back
to Eritrea. Some were also deported to Malta. They went straight to
prison and were forced to confess and say, "I betrayed my country."

This TV program instilled great fear in Meron and his peers. But it was
the brutality of the military camps that was the source of his motivation
to ultimately flee the dictatorship.

The first six months, we accepted this military training. There's a lot
of punishment but we were kind of okay with it. But when school
started, that treatment didn't change. Unexpectedly, they would tie
your hands. At times we were told to stand in the sun, in extreme heat,
without moving for half an hour or an hour. People would drop to the
ground fainting. Or they would tell you just to get on the ground, make

you crawl, and beat you with sticks. They tied my hands to my legs behind me. My face was on the ground. Hands and legs tied by my bed curtain on a hot sunny day in the open air.

Sometimes there was no meaning to it, why they did it. Many times, the person in charge, if he was angry, he would do it. They had all this power over you, and those people hadn't seen enough salary for a very long time. They didn't get enough breaks, so that also ran into their head. So, they had their own psychological issues. They took their anger out on you.

We learned to accept it as part of our life. But what are you going to become if that's how they treat you? A productive citizen? How are you going to think out of the box? How are you going to create? How are you going to lead a nation? By the way, the government leaders, they also sent their children to the military training camp, but every weekend they got to go on holiday. Some leaders came and took them for better treatment somewhere else.

Meron started to explore possible ways to leave the military camp. He knew there was an active shoot-to-kill policy on the border. A number of his own friends had been shot in their attempt to escape. But he knew he had to get out of this nightmare. So, he was patient and planned his escape. During a two-week break from the military, he devised a strategy that considered what border to cross and who to go with (someone who spoke Arabic for the border crossing into Sudan), how to get some money, and the best time to leave. He could not tell his mother about his plans, which was the most difficult part.

The Escape

After his break, he arrived back at the camp at 5:00 P.M., and the next day, at 10:00 A.M., he and five friends left on foot, carrying only a few supplies. First, they had to get past the military checkpoint. But they knew the soldiers on duty, so when they told them they were just going to the nearby town for some supplies, the soldiers trusted them to return quickly. When Meron and his friends got outside the view of the soldiers, one by one they moved toward the bushes and hid. When the sun started to disappear, their journey began. For the most part, they traveled the entire night, out into the unknown, with little money or supplies. At first they walked, looking for the next bush that would provide cover, but at night they would jog. They occasionally ran into tribal people and asked if they were going the right way to Sudan. Then they would run off again under cover of night. They had little appetite for food for fear of being caught.

After a journey of twenty-four hours, they crossed into Sudan and the next day they were captured by the Sudanese military, who gave them food and drink. The military sent them to the nearby city of Kassala. After their names were recorded, they were sent to the Wad Sharefay refugee camp, where they remained for about two weeks with little water or food. At the camp, Meron connected with hundreds of other Eritreans who had fled the military, and heard horrific stories about those who had been captured.

He was then moved to an open refugee camp called Sita WoEshrin, where he saw Eritreans who had been there for many years, some for decades, living in squalor. He decided that his best way out was to get to Khartoum, the capital of Sudan. Meron had some money he had hidden in the belt section of his pants for emergencies. He used some of it to call one of his uncles in South Africa, who made arrangements to help him. He got a smuggler to take Meron during the night in the back of a small Toyota. Meron spent seven months in Khartoum.

They put me in a hotel, and my uncle paid for the expenses and it was only then I started thinking, What's next? My uncle said, "Well, you want to study, right? Then I think education is possible here in South Africa."

A lot of my friends were going to Libya, and from Libya to Italy and then to England and all sorts of places, so it was very tempting, but I always had that dream of education and that's the only thing I knew my parents would want me to do. This Libya and Mediterranean crossing was not for me. If I could go to South Africa and get an education, that's it, yeah, so that's it.

With the help of his uncle, and by bribing immigration officials, he secured a safe way to exit the country for South Africa. He boarded the first flight of his life at age nineteen, where he flew on a forged visa to Dubai.

In Dubai, he was inspired by the skyscrapers that made him dream of getting an engineering degree, but after a few weeks he became deeply depressed by the many Eritrean and Ethiopian girls who had been sold as sex slaves and were there working as prostitutes. He knew he had to get out. More bribes were paid, and finally he got a ticket to Mozambique, where he could not get out of the airport without paying yet another bribe. After hiding in a hotel for three days, he was picked up by another smuggler who drove him and three others to the South African border. The driver was armed with a small pistol. He went to the immigration office with the four men's passports and got them stamped with entry visas. Finally, Meron arrived in Cape Town by bus from Johannesburg.

Becoming an Activist in South Africa

His uncle, also a student, and not a person of great means, managed to find the money to help Meron make the perilous journey from Sudan. He had borrowed money from friends to help Meron pursue his dream of reaching South Africa for a good education.

"I do this for you not to pay me back, but I want it to be for your parents, for your siblings," he told me. He made a lot of sacrifices for me. And so my new life began. But my uncle only helped me to get to South Africa. I had to pay my education by working as a waiter every night and double shifts on weekends.

So, with minimal resources and no knowledge of English, Meron first applied for asylum so that he could work and study. He worked as a carpenter and later as a waiter to pay for his engineering studies. The waiter job not only taught him English but also exposed him to many people and ideas that would shape his life. He enrolled in college to complete a certificate degree. With his high grades, he was then ready to apply to a university, which he entered the following year. For five years, Meron led a busy life working and studying. He rented a room next to his workplace in a middle-class neighborhood. In the restaurant, he met many great people who later became close friends and mentors.

Things were getting worse in Eritrea, and like his uncle who had brought him to safety, Meron brought his older brother to South Africa. But he could not forget his experiences in the military and refugee camps, the running, the endless bribing, and the fear of never getting anywhere to improve his life.

I started to question myself a lot. It was like, I am lucky, I got the chance to study and get paid well. But there were a lot of people dying every day. That might have been my fate. And I think I took it very personally and I started asking, What can I do? At some point I remember asking all sorts of people, Why is it like this, what does life mean? I started asking psychiatrists, professors, pastors, you name it, all sorts of people who might have a better understanding about the meaning of life and there wasn't anyone who could give me something tangible. Something I wanted to hear.

Being a refugee in South Africa was a big issue. In 2008, I couldn't leave my home for two weeks because they were killing people, foreigners. It was easier for a foreign white person to be respected in South Africa than it was for me, a black person in my own continent. They killed dozens of African people that year in the most horrific way. They killed them by covering them in gasoline and lighting a fire, or by using a machete, like what you saw in Rwanda, or by stoning them.

So, I got involved with a human rights advocacy group started by former students. They called it Eritrean Movement for Democracy and Human Rights.

Then I was about twenty-four and I also worked with other refugees helping them to study at a university so that they would advocate for their own communities. We made sure those refugees got their asylum papers processed on time and helped them continue at the university by providing or securing scholarships. It was called Unity for Tertiary Refugee Students.

It gave me a sense of meaning, I was helping and I was doing something. I could not actually go to Sudan or Libya and save these people, but I could do something where I was in South Africa.

In 2012, Meron was invited to be a keynote speaker at the One Young World Human Rights Plenary in Pittsburgh, where 1,300 people would be in attendance. But he was unsure whether he could get a visa and whether the visa would be accepted by the immigration officer at the airport. But he tried and had to fly back and forth from Cape Town to Johannesburg many times, bribing his way through the red tape. Once, he could not get a train to Pretoria and had to spend the night studying in the airport coffee shop. Immigration officials entered, and he got into a long conversation with one of them, sharing his story. He was told it was really a matter of luck depending on who the immigration official was on duty at the airport at the time. Two months later, Meron was at the Johannesburg International Airport about to go through customs to board the flight for the conference, and he approached the official with great trepidation.

I realized all of a sudden that it was the same guy who told me that you have to be lucky. It was the same guy, and he was laughing at me, I was laughing at him and he looked at me and said, "You see how small the world is?" And then he said to me, "Just don't forget me when you become big leader," and he stamped my visa. "Go," he said.

It just happened, I never even bought this guy a cup of coffee.

This is how Meron concluded his speech, while dressed in traditional Eritrean white garb, at the conference in Pittsburgh:

Accommodate a refugee inside your community, your country, your government. Recognize the value that refugees bring into making a country multicultural. I feel compelled to close my speech by encouraging you to be part of the solution. The hope of any refugee is to live a useful, peaceful and happy life somewhere in the world, just as you.

Leaving a Life Behind

It was in Pittsburgh that Meron's life changed again. At the conference he met many people who encouraged him to stay in the United States and seek asylum. He had friends in the San Francisco Bay area, so perhaps, he thought, it would be possible. But it was an agonizing decision. In South Africa he had a good professional job with a solid income. He was also in a master's program in transportation planning. Yet his Eritrean passport was expiring soon, and there was growing xenophobia there about refugees. If he decided to stay in the United States, he knew he would lose everything he had worked so hard for in South Africa and would have to start anew.

But he felt that the United States provided more protection for refugees. So, he made the courageous decision to stay. He settled in Oakland, where there were many Eritrean refugees, and hired an immigration attorney. It took a year for Meron, unable to work or study, to finally get asylum status.

Eventually, Meron got a job working in a 7-Eleven and began the process of shaping a new life in a place he never imagined living, while sending money to his younger brother so that he could escape to South Africa. He spent the next years working a variety of jobs, including taxi driver, and continuing his activism. He yearned to get back to his education, and he learned about the University of San Francisco (USF) and its social justice mission to change the world.

Wherever I went, I lost a year or two to adapt. When I was in South Africa, I wasted a year to adapt to the life. And then I came to the USA, and I needed two years of my life to adapt here. So you waste time as a refugee every time you move to a new place. And you keep getting older. But once again, there's that word. Hope. I think that hope is the only thing that keeps you going. That's what kept me going, but also wanting something more. I wanted education badly. As a refugee, as an immigrant, I have to bring something more to the table. I cannot just show talent.

In 2015, having been granted only a minimal scholarship, Meron entered the master's degree program in international studies at USF while continuing to work as a taxi driver and speaking at refugee conferences around the world, including in Thailand, in Canada, and throughout North America. He started an organization, Student Outreach for Refugees, Asylees and Immigrants, and organized a conference on human rights celebrating the twenty-fifth anniversary of Eritrean independence. He stayed in frequent contact with his mother in Eritrea and his two brothers in Canada.

I work with refugees and I encourage them that they have a dream. I want them to choose something, to have the need, the want, the desire. "I want to be this." And if there is that, that is the starting point. The next question is how do you get there? And that is my message. Have the hope. Have the want. And I think for many refugees, it's that hope that keeps them alive.

Meron was deeply moved to be selected as the USF graduation speaker in December 2016, the first refugee given that honor. One could hear a pin drop in the crowded room when, during his speech, he presented to USF president Paul Fitzgerald the International Refugee flag. Meron was beaming with joy. The only sadness was that his mom was denied a visa to come to the United States to see her son graduate and give his inspiring speech.

Meron is a man on a mission to change the world and its treatment of refugees. He is filled with hope, but that hope is mixed with realism. Since his graduation, Meron has been writing his memoir and he often lectures on the situation of refugees and Eritreans in particular. He is also studying for the LSAT and hopes to attend law school in the next few years. Meron is currently working as an assistant at an immigration law firm in Berkeley. Meron is dedicated to bringing about change in Eritrea that will lead his country to democracy, where human rights will be upheld and people can live in freedom. This is his utmost priority.

Anyone who knows Meron is confident that he will find the path that will lead him to have an impact on this world.

The time for us to wait for champions of our causes to come from overseas are over. We should be the 'captains of our fate' and cultivate our champions, for no one understands our fears, aspiration and nightmares. There are young Madibas amongst us that will lead us in this journey. Let us give them the chance to fulfill our promise of a better, peaceful and prosperous Africa.

(From "Big Shoes and Youthful Feet," *Huffington Post*, December 23, 2013, an article Meron wrote reflecting on Nelson Mandela's death.)

CHAPTER 2

NOEMI PEREZ-LEMUS

GUATEMALA

My father sympathized with the revolution. He always talked about
the people who fought for our country. He could remember them all.
He gave his children their names. He wanted us to always remember
our country and the people who tried to save it.

The Central American country of Guatemala has experienced extreme
upheaval since its 1524 colonization by Spain. In the twentieth century, this
unrest was exacerbated by military coups, civil wars, environmental
degradation, and mass starvation. The legacy of these experiences followed
Guatemala into the twenty-first century. It has some of the highest rates
of inequality in the world and remains plagued by poverty, malnutrition,
and crime. These problems also contributed to a refugee crisis and the
internal displacement of millions of people. Many of Guatemala's problems stem from the involvement of the United States and its efforts to stave
off the growth of power of left-leaning Communist regimes during the
Cold War and throughout the post–Cold War era.

The United States' Cold War policy had a devastating impact on Guatemala. The American corporation the United Fruit Company (UFC) controlled a sizable portion of the arable land in Guatemala where it
cultivated fruit for the U.S. domestic market. Guatemalan workers had
horrific working conditions. But in 1951, Jacobo Árbenz was democratically
elected as president and vowed to help improve the quality of life for workers throughout the country. Árbenz instituted reforms in working conditions and seized some UFC land. The UFC used its political clout to
petition the Eisenhower administration to act against the left-leaning government. In 1954, President Eisenhower instructed the CIA to orchestrate
a coup. Árbenz's government was overthrown and a series of U.S.-backed
military dictators assumed control of the country.

These dictators orchestrated a terror campaign that led to the displacement of millions and the deaths of thousands. In 1960, left-wing guerilla
groups, predominantly made up of ethnic Mayans and peasants, began

fighting the right-wing government. It marked the beginning of the thirty-six-year Guatemalan Civil War. The U.S.-backed government received assistance from the CIA and U.S. Special Forces in creating an effective security apparatus that monitored and targeted thousands with a commitment to exterminating anyone deemed an "enemy" of the state. Throughout the 1980s, counterinsurgency activities by the military and paramilitary groups focused on systematically eradicating the Mayan populace in the highlands in what came to be known as the "Silent Holocaust." These "death squads" murdered about 166,000 Mayans along with 34,000 peasants during the Civil War. Some 200,000 Guatemalans fled to neighboring Mexico, more than 1 million Mayans were internally displaced, and 45,917 Guatemalans immigrated to the United States in 1989. Today, Guatemala remains mired in political corruption, human rights violations, and gang warfare.

Meeting Noemi Perez-Lemus and listening to her powerful story about the Guatemala that she and her family called home and cherished, and ultimately had to flee, provided me with great insight into the horrific human rights violations that have taken place in her home country.

Her beautiful home in Los Angeles is filled with art reflecting her pride in Guatemalan culture. She has prepared a gracious snack of plantains, mango, and *pepetoria* (pumpkin seeds). She and her husband, Oscar, make me feel at home with their warmth. One can tell that she has trepidation about telling her story. Each time she tells it, she must relive it. Noemi walks me through her story in perfect English, but as we go into the painful parts she uses more Spanish. Her eyes fill with tears as the memories come flooding back.

I leave Noemi with a heavy but expansive heart. It is difficult to fathom that we live in a world where humans are treated like Noemi. But, ultimately, the ability to triumph over evil is Noemi's story. The ability to celebrate life and make the most of it is Noemi's story. The ability to shape a life of meaning and give so much to the United States reflects Noemi's commitment and perseverance. She will never take for granted the refuge she received in America and hopes that many more will be granted political asylum.

Children Who Returned from a Walk through Hell

It is important for me to contribute to peace and justice in the world and offer my solidarity and speak out for our rights. We must speak out. If we don't our rights will be taken away, and there are so many rights that are in danger, like immigration, issues about women, Latinos and blacks. In Guatemala, the struggles that they are going through are so powerful. My heart will always be in my motherland.

Deep Family Roots

Noemi was born in 1963 in Guatemala City, Guatemala. Her father was a shoemaker and her mother worked in a school. The middle child of five, Noemi grew up poor in a house passed down from her grandparents. It had water and electricity but little else. But she was conscious, even at a young age, that there were people who had even less than she.

We were very close to the very poor neighborhood. We were poor, but they were poorer. The limonadas. Their houses were very basic. Not houses even. They were simple shelters covered in plastic, no water or power, and there was a lot of crime.

I had a very close relationship with my grandparents, especially with my grandmother. Then she died when I was seven years old. My grandfather had died two years before. My mom and my dad always worked, and we were happy when they came home. I loved it when my mom cooked and took us to the market.

I was in childcare for four years. I started public school in the first grade. Our parents had to provide all our school supplies. The government didn't give anything, so we had to buy it. Parents had to buy the uniform, the book, the notebook, the pencils.

Noemi learned a great deal from her parents. Her dad, Jose Domingo Perez, was involved in social causes, and she went to marches from an early age. They marched for workers' rights, for change in the government, and for human rights and social justice. Her mom, Celia Diomicio, was a strong woman and early feminist who had the courage to leave her troubled childhood home and venture out on her own at an early age. She worked hard and provided for her children.

> *But then, in 1977, the earthquake happened. It was a 7.5 and everything was destroyed. It was bad for everyone in Guatemala. They closed the school where my mom was working, so my mom had to decide what to do. For a couple months, she worked in the kitchen of a French restaurant. She started saving money, and she thought if she had the courage to leave us with my father, she would go to the U.S. to save us by making even more money. My mom. Just her. She had one friend in the U.S. So, my mom asked her friend if she would accept her. She saved money, and she borrowed some money, and then she left us.*
>
> *The plan was that she'd be gone for one or two years and see if she could save money and come back. It was traumatic. In the beginning, we cried a lot. I didn't feel that she abandoned us. I knew that she had to move for economic reasons, economic hardship. But when we took her to the bus station, we cried, and we cried for so many days after.*
>
> *When she left she told us that you must have an education, you always have to work hard. We must have a better life. This is what her dream was for us.*
>
> *She went to Torrance, near Los Angeles. She started working in a factory, and cleaning houses. She had two jobs, to send us money to have a better life in Guatemala.*

They had lost their home in the earthquake, and the country lay in ruins. Celia was an economic refugee by necessity. She did not want to leave but had no choice and was one of many people forced to enter the United States without legal documents.

Noemi, at age twelve, and her siblings had to play a role in taking care of their new house (a prefab), cooking, and paying the bills—everything her mom had done. Her dad worked long hours. Well before cell phones, they arranged for a monthly call with her mom. Celia kept telling her family from Los Angeles, "You have to be strong."

Noemi started middle school. She experienced injustices firsthand—there were no books, no desks, and no teachers for months at a time. The students learned to organize and tried to appeal to the school authorities and the government. They took to the streets to protest their plight. This situation continued into her high school years. She began to hear about students who had disappeared or had been killed, such as Robin Garcia, the student activist who had been tortured and was found dead with his fingers cut off and his eyes cut out. He was the same age as Noemi, and thus she became deeply committed to the fight against injustice.

The students' cause was joined by people living in poverty and by workers who received slave wages with no benefits. The marches and protests continued. The government grew more violent. On January 31, 1980, thirty-six students and peasants died in a fire at the Spanish embassy.

> *Then, teachers from the university, teachers from the high school, were killed. People who just said anything against the government, they were killed. They started killing, killing, killing. We marched when the mayor of Guatemala City was killed.*
>
> *Then it happened to us. One day in May 1982, my brother, Marvyn, who was only fourteen at the time, went to play basketball at the same court he played at every day and he didn't come home. That was when the nightmare started for us.*

Haunted by Screams

Her brother always returned at 3:00 P.M., so on this day when he did not show, the family was immediately worried. Noemi went to look for him at the *cancha* (basketball court), at his school, and at his friends' homes. Marvyn played on the Guatemalan national junior basketball team, so they checked every *cancha*. The days ahead would include daily searches of hospitals, morgues, and jails. Marvyn was nowhere to be found. Such disappearances were becoming more frequent in Guatemala, but no one thought it would happen to them.

Three nights later, Noemi and her sister Lissette were still looking all over for their brother. They took buses throughout the city searching for him. As they were returning to their bus stop, they saw that the street was filled with police cars. So, they got off at the next stop, hoping to avoid the police.

> *But many police cars surrounded us. Police, and the army. They stopped us. We were very frightened. Then, someone yelled, "Take them." We started screaming. That was my only weapon, to scream, and let people know that this was happening. There were people and cars everywhere, everybody watching when they took us. I start screaming so loudly. It's like you have all this adrenaline that comes out to help you survive. People came out of their homes and their businesses. What I wanted in this madness was for people to see that I was being taken away. That is the last thing I recall that night, as I was then hit on the head.*

The sisters woke up at what they thought was the national police station, where they were accused of being guerrillas and ordered to give up names or be tortured. In the torture area they finally saw their brother. Noemi was thrilled to find him alive but would have rather died than face torture herself. She was beaten, violated, and brutalized. She was thrown back into a room with seven other students, all of whom were suffering. They had no water and no food. They lacked the energy to talk, so they just cried as they lay on the floor holding each other.

She thought her torturers were secret police because they wore no uniforms. Noemi knew that many people had already been killed. Her only hope was for her suffering to end.

There are no words to describe the anguish—the physical pain from the torture, the emotional pain of knowing that my parents were out looking for me, the pain of knowing that there was no hope.

Noemi's torture went on for days. They put masking tape on her hands and covered her face with newspaper and tape, then tossed her and the other students into a van. At that terrible moment she was just hoping for death.

These people, I don't know what they were, but they were not human beings. How could they be? They tortured us and yelled terrible things at us day and night. I will never forget the screams coming day and night from the torture rooms. They will haunt me my whole life.

Finally, after many days of torture and deprivation, a group of men told Noemi and the others that they would be released if they signed this agreement: you were never tortured, you were simply detained for questioning, you are part of the guerrilla movement. There was no question for Noemi and her friends that they would sign. They were also told that the next day a television crew would film their testimony. After they agreed, they were cleaned up by a doctor, given food, and allowed to shower so that they would look presentable for the cameras. Noemi felt they were being released because of the relentless pressure of her father, who went to newspapers and radio stations every day, and her mother, who had flown home when her children initially disappeared, as well as from Amnesty International and other groups. On June 10, 1982, she and seventeen others were released. Originally there were three more in captivity: one was tortured to death and two of them had disappeared, probably killed or taken somewhere else.

For the next three months she and her family remained in hiding. They moved in rural areas almost daily until arrangements were made to smuggle them out of the country. Filled with fear, they never knew when the nightmare might start again.

With money her mother had saved, Noemi, her dad, and her siblings were smuggled illegally into the United States from Mexico in 1982. They endured a long journey hiding in the back of trucks, in stifling heat with little water for about ten days. Finally, they were reunited in Los Angeles. But shortly after arriving, Noemi was picked up by immigration and sent back to Mexico. In Tijuana, her mother managed to get her money and she was again smuggled across the border.

Acclimating to a New Life

In Los Angeles, living in a two-bedroom apartment with her parents and four siblings, Noemi got a job with her mom at a microchip factory during the day and went to high school at night. Even though the family was living with so little, they no longer worried about a repressive regime taking them away. Her dad got a job working the night shift at Winchell's Donuts, and her older siblings were also employed. Things appeared good.

And then, her mom died.

While at work with her mother on April 27, 1983, a co-worker came to tell Noemi that her mom had had a stroke and was taken away in an ambulance. Celia, just forty-six, died two days later. The family was inconsolable. Their anchor was gone. Noemi wondered if the years of stress, worry, and hard work contributed to her death.

> *Again, we had to continue life without her. She had given us strength. She had given us so much power that we said to each other, "We must continue." I didn't go to school, I went back to work. Sometimes working two shifts at the factory. If they said, "We need you to stay," I stayed and worked Saturdays, too.*

Soon Noemi became connected with the Guatemalan Information Center. Here she met many other refugees and stayed informed about the situation in her native country. In the early 1980s the center had many events in LA to raise funds as the situation had only worsened in Guatemala. One million people had been displaced, tens of thousands of refugees were living in makeshift camps in Mexico, and the government was bombing many parts of the country. Noemi and others did their best to raise money to send to the people for food and shelter.

Through the 1980s, we were working for Guatemala here in the United States, organizing marches and protests in Los Angeles against the intervention of the U.S. into Guatemala and El Salvador and Nicaragua. We were trying to educate people and to tell Congress about what is going on in Guatemala and building solidarity with Guatemalan people, refugees. People were still disappearing, people were looking for their families. Also, at the same time, the U.S. government was giving money to those governments, even though they knew of the many human rights violations.

Noemi was grateful to be in America and for what this country made possible for her. However, she could not shy away from criticizing the government and especially its activities at that time in Guatemala, El Salvador, and Nicaragua. The United States supported the military regimes. However, Noemi had no difficulty distinguishing the goodness of the American people from the foreign policy makers.

Noemi was working in factories as well as cleaning houses, babysitting, and doing anything she could to support herself and her family. In 1984, she met her future husband, Oscar, who shared a similar history, at one of the activist events. They married a year later.

In 1985, through her many contacts, Noemi met two nuns who were starting a center to help refugees in Vista, California. She joined them, and they started Listo (Spanish for "ready"), which helped Latin refugees and immigrants learn English and basic work skills and provided them with insights about shaping a life in America. Noemi still was not a U.S. citizen at this point. In 1986, she applied for political asylum. It would be a long journey to citizenship. The United States was granting less than one half of a percent of Guatemalans political asylum.

But no one wanted to take the case because it was too complicated. This was hard. Even though we had all the proof about what happened, they would say, it's difficult and they don't want to take on a case they were going to lose. Or one that was going to take five years. Also, some people thought that maybe it's dangerous, given what was still going on with Guatemala and the U.S. Finally, Niels Nelson, with public counsel in Los Angeles, took our family's case.

Once again, the strength that she had received from her mother got her through the five years it took to attain refugee status. It was an expensive proposition with attorneys, depositions, and extensive written materials. But the United States granted her refugee status, which is the doorway to citizenship.

In 1997, after ten years of working as community organizers and advocates, she and Oscar started a tax consulting business. They now have four employees. Oscar also helps people with immigration issues, while Noemi remains very involved in the situation in Guatemala, which is terrible. She describes it as overrun with drugs, gangs, and poverty.

Noemi took general education courses and studied business at night at several community colleges in the Los Angeles area. She would have liked to graduate from college but could never afford the time or the money.

First, we had to move from our birth country because of the horrible political situation. This is not what we wanted. In my case, I'm a refugee for political reasons. My husband and my mother are refugees for economic reasons. We did not want to run from our country, but we had to for survival. When you come to another country, it's hard, because you don't know the language, you don't know the laws, you don't know the culture, you don't know the ways to work the system. It is very hard, and it takes a lot of patience and perseverance.

When we came to the U.S., my mom told us, "This is your new country, and you have to embrace life here." We know that there are many things that this country did to our country, but it's not the people, it's the government. There are a lot of nice people here, in the U.S., who open their hearts, their homes. Still, there is a lot of hate, there is a lot of xenophobia, there is a lot of discrimination. Every day I have to fight that.

Even though she and Oscar are American citizens who contribute a great deal to the country, she feels that discrimination continues. Ten years ago, they moved into the Northridge house, where they still reside, in LA's San Fernando Valley. While moving in, they were reminded that they were the only Latino family in this Caucasian area when a neighbor told them "Turn off that f—n' Mexican music." These incidents do not seem to faze her, but they must take a toll.

The tears will always be with Noemi, but joy is on her face. She and Oscar have now been married for thirty-three years and have two grown children.

One of my daughters graduated in May 2018 from Cal State LA. Her major was Latin America studies with a minor in women, gender, and sexuality studies. She is now applying to various doctoral programs in ethnic studies. My other daughter works in the family business and will be returning to school in the fall of 2019 to study economics and social enterprise.

My childhood life was hard. I went through hard times, my mother had to immigrate to the U.S. to help us to have a better life. I am a torture survivor, but that experience made me strong, a lifetime fighter. I am happy, I am alive. I have a family who I love, and they love me, my husband, my children, my father, my sisters and my brothers. I have a job, a home.

Because I am a survivor, it is more powerful, and I am more grateful to be alive. Every day I give thanks to the universe, mother earth and my ancestors to have been given another day to be on this planet with my family and do the things that I love to do.

CHAPTER 3

ASINJA BADEEL

IRAQ AND THE YAZIDIS

As a child, I saw the world outside of Iraq as very far away. I thought
that living in a safe land, freedom, security and happiness were
unachievable for me. How could a young female from a small old
minority like Yazidi reach the other side of the world, where all the
dreams are possible?

One of the many victims of the chaos and violence in Iraq is Asinja Badeel.
Like the stories of so many other Iraqis, hers is multifaceted. It is the story
of Iraq's destruction, the pain of war, the genocide against the Yazidi
people, and deep personal anguish. It is a story of a girl whose imagination allowed her to see outside of her small Iraqi village into a world where
people are free. It is a story of a woman with a keen intellect, a compassionate heart, and the determination to keep going. It is a story of shattered dreams and courage.

Many will never forget the haunting pictures that permeated the media
in early August 2014 of the 50,000 Yazidi people who were trapped by ISIS
(Islamic State of Iraq and Syria) on Mount Sinjar in northern Iraq. The
United States reacted with airstrikes allowing most of the people to be
evacuated.

Iraq has been plagued with violence for most of the twenty-first century.
The United States' invasion in 2003 and the subsequent fall of Saddam
Hussein created a power struggle that has consumed the country. Sectar-
ian violence has resulted in the rise of extremist groups such as ISIS and
ushered in an invigorated Kurdish independence movement. These elements, coupled with the United States' military withdrawal, created a
struggle for power that diminished the government's power and authority. Iraq is a country in turmoil where the chaos and lack of government
leadership has led to continued violence. This void enabled ISIS to capture a significant portion of the country, which resulted in the persecution and extermination of minority groups. The attempted destruction of
the Yazidi people has been labeled "genocide" by the United States and

other countries (the only time that term has been used except in the context of Rwanda and Darfur).

The Yazidis are an ethnic and religious minority living predominantly in Iraq and Syria. They are indigenous to Mesopotamia, and their religion—Yazidism, which has many commonalities with Zoroastrianism—is one of the oldest religions in the world. The Yazidis and their religion are endogamous, which means that one must be born as a Yazidi; one cannot become a Yazidi by converting to Yazidism. The group has been persecuted for centuries, but until recently, it has lived primarily in obscurity. In August 2014, ISIS began a targeted campaign of terror and extermination against the Iraqi Yazidi population. ISIS believes that the Yazidis are "devil worshippers," so they razed their villages, executed hundreds of Yazidi males, enslaved hundreds of their women, and forced thousands to flee to Mount Sinjar. Once the Yazidis were trapped on Mount Sinjar, the international media devoted significant airtime to their plight until Kurdish Peshmerga forces saved them. It is estimated that over 10,000 Yazidis were killed or kidnapped by ISIS in the month of August 2014. Thousands of Yazidis have been killed or enslaved since then, and the genocide against them continues to be perpetrated by ISIS.

In this chapter about Asinja and her journey, one sees the unfolding of a life from a village in Iraq to Houston, Texas. As I sat with her in her office, it was clear that Asinja is a determined woman who wants to continue to pursue her learning and contribute to life in her new country. She also remains passionately committed to the plight of the Yazidi people.

The Imaginary Girl

My grandfather would tell us stories. I keep them in my mind because forgetting what happened is exactly what they want—for us to disappear completely.

Asinja's journey began in the small village of Bashiqa on the Ninawa Plain in northern Iraq, a beautiful region filled with olive trees and green valleys, with Mount Sinjar in the distance. From the time of her birth, her grandfather Badeel was a vital force in her life. It was he who rejected traditional Yazidi names for her and instead gave her the name Asinja, after a Norse goddess of wisdom and love.

One of eight children, Asinja was raised in a small, two-bedroom house where she and her three brothers and four sisters shared a single room. Her father, Nawaf, was a dentist and her mother, Ghazala, took care of the children and household, and harvested and sold olives and chamomile. But it was her grandfather, a religious leader and successful businessman, who filled Asinja with the pride, curiosity, and courage that would sustain her throughout her life.

At the core of her family life was their Yazidi identity. Yazidis are considered a Kurdish-speaking ethno-religious minority. However, in Bashiqa the language was Arabic. Badeel taught Asinja about Yazidi history, culture, and way of life as well as about the massacres they endured over the centuries. Monotheists who believe in the power of nature and the goodness of people, they would say five daily prayers, asking for peace and safety, focusing on the oneness of nature, particularly the sun, which they view as the source of energy for the world and ultimate truth. Twice a year, Yazidis from all over gathered in nearby Lalish, home to the holiest temple of their faith.

But because of the violent history of Sunni Muslim persecution against the Yazidis, Asinja's parents did not want her to make her identity known to people outside of the community.

The Muslims consider us infidels and accuse us of not worshiping God. They killed us many times through history and every time they destroyed our culture, our temples and our books. They killed our most educated people, so that we didn't want to talk about our religion anymore. My mother told me to say I am Yazidi, but nothing more. My grandfather said not to write anything down because if we document what we are worshiping, they will kill us for sure.

That is why Yazidi women and men are not allowed to marry from another religion. If you marry a Yazidi man who was born as a Yazidi, our blood will continue.

As a young child, Asinja attended the public elementary school, where she excelled. Eager to learn, she was often named *qutwat al Saaf,* "the role model," with the best grades and the most respect of her classmates.

As she grew up, she began to understand the damage inflicted on the people of Iraq by Saddam Hussein.

We all lived in fear of him and what he might do at any time. He kept the Iraqi people isolated from the world. Anyone who dissented was killed. But at the time I was a kid learning English and watching Oprah because she talked, and I just listened and I loved the topics that she was talking about. Then when I reached high school, my father thought that I was ready to read books that he was reading. I had three or four books in English. The first I read was Gone with the Wind. *And I read it again in Arabic because I was worried I missed something. Then* Love in the Time of Cholera *by Gabriel García Márquez. I read that one four times.*

Marquez transformed me from the reality of my life to his story. There were a lot of times that I didn't like this life, in this place where I was so limited, not like the Western girls my age who were traveling, doing a lot of things that I couldn't do. I saw a lot of barriers in my life, so I watched movies, like Rain Man, *and learned English, read books and tried to isolate myself from the life in Bashiqa and just be*

part of this Western life. I wanted to educate myself about the West-
ern world and the only window we had was through art and movies.

That's why they called me The Imaginary Girl.

I talked a lot about what I imagined about the other side of the
world. But everyone told me that Saddam would never let us travel
to the United States. I was told that the only place I would be is in
Bashiqa because I have to marry a Yazidi man. And my education
has to be within this border, too. Though my father supported my
desire to attend college, my mom didn't think I would be allowed to
go to the University of Mosul. Very few girls were able to, and it was
only because they had family there. For most Yazidi girls, there was
high school and that's it. So you stay in the village and you think
about marriage. For two reasons. The woman's place is only in the
house, doing the house chores and all of that. The other reason is
because you are Yazidi and if you went to a Muslim city, it would be
dangerous. When I graduated from high school, in 2001, my mom
and oldest brother told me that I could not go to Mosul because it
was not safe and we couldn't afford it.

The Terror of Saddam

When Asinja was still a child, in the early 1990s, she would listen to her
father and his friends talk about Saddam with hatred and fear. Military
service was mandatory for Iraqi men. But Asinja's father did not want to
serve Saddam, so he had not joined the army during the war with Iran.
Now they were after him.

If a man did not serve in the army or special forces, Saddam's men
would come after the woman and kids and they came a lot to our
house. It was a terrifying experience. I remember one time they came
to Bashiqa and took many families to our mountain and they buried
them alive because their men hadn't served.

Sometimes Saddam's guards would go to the University of Mosul, and other areas of northern Ninewa, because it was known that they have the most beautiful women there. They would grab the women by force and rape them.

My mother and I would go to the forest to collect wood to make bread. One day we returned to find Saddam's police attacking our house, flipping chairs, throwing clothes.

They were looking for my dad and cousins. I saw my cousin, Zuhair, running away from them to the forest. They shot at him with guns, but they couldn't catch him.

But they got my dad. He was in his pajamas. They wanted my oldest brother too. My mom begged them, "He's just a student and he's not old enough for the army." They threw my brother down and they took my dad. They put him in a car and took him to jail.

The facility was Badush jail, where they put the north people, as they called us. Many of the men there died. We don't know if they killed themselves or if the soldiers killed them. There was torture. Since no international people were coming to see this jail, no one knew about it, so they could do anything they wanted to do.

Two years later, Saddam offered Alafo alaam, a general forgiveness for all prisoners. I think because it was the end of the war and Iraq had won, he was celebrating. It was the evening when my dad came home. My mom didn't know he was coming. He just entered the house and looked so old and tired. He was hungry. And he was so depressed that he couldn't work for a very long time after, putting my mom under a lot of pressure.

The Iran war, the Kuwait war, the U.S. war, all took a lot from my dreams, but they could not take away my hope. That hope was stronger than the Iraqi dictator, brighter than the flames of the bombings and explosions, and clearer than the smoke that darkened the skies of Baghdad.

Anyone Killed for Any Reason

Asinja met her future husband, Saher, right after high school. Born and raised in Baghdad, he came to Bashiqa to purchase products, including olives from Asinja's mom, for his father's business. As Saher and Asinja got to know each other, she made it clear that pursuing her studies was critical to her. Like her father, he supported her dreams of higher education. The parents then met to arrange the marriage.

Asinja and Saher were married in 2001. They moved to Baghdad to start their life together, living with his parents. Asinja was inspired by the city, its energy and people, and felt there was much opportunity for her. She tried to enroll in the university but did not have access to her high school transcripts or records. By the time she had everything in order she learned she was pregnant.

That is life in Iraq—marriage and then children right away. I felt like I kept postponing my dreams. When I became pregnant, I was sick for months. But when my son came I was so happy and I started to love the time that I was spending with him. We decided I could go study while I was living with my mother-in-law who could take care of the baby while I was in school.

Then suddenly the war, this time with the United States, and things started to get darker. In 2003, they told us to move from Baghdad because it had become too dangerous. The only safe place was Bashiqa. It was 3:00 A.M. on March 18th, just the day before my birthday, and in two cars, with my husband's family, we fled from Baghdad. It was a six-hour drive to Bashiqa. We could hear the fighter jets. The United States had a center in Turkey and we were very close. We heard when they came and hit Mosul.

After forty-five days, we saw the United States army. They came in their big trucks to the village and I remember that the people welcomed them. The kids were running after them. They were giving candies to

the kids. They told us there would be a new face for Iraq. We will know
freedom. We will be able to travel. We will be able to have a lot of
Western products, like the internet, phones, newspapers, TV news.

The people were ecstatic that the dictator was out of power and the
country they loved could be rebuilt. A few months later, Asinja, Saher, and
the baby returned with his family to Baghdad. But life was not what they
had expected.

Baghdad had been torn apart. There was no job for my husband. The
university was not open. We were supported by my in-laws. No more
Hussein, but no one knew what to do.

After nearly a year, her husband landed a job with an American security company. They now had some money and could start to live again. In
2004, Asinja was pregnant with their second child, who was born in 2005.
She decided to start school when it reopened in the fall.

That dream was, once again, shattered.

Baghdad again was in total chaos, buildings destroyed, bodies everywhere. Militias were fighting, there was terrible conflict between Shia and
Sunni Muslims, and there was no law or order.

They killed everyone. Every day there were bombings. We actually
were getting used to life with dead bodies lying on the streets. Anyone
could be killed for any reason.

Then my husband received a frightening warning—a bullet
wrapped in a piece of paper with his name and a simple message. You
will be killed. They saw any Iraqi working with American companies
as a traitor. And the fact that he was Yazidi made it even more
dangerous.

But my husband didn't stop working because we really needed the
income. My father had an idea. He suggested that I take a very quick
course to be a teacher, which I did and was soon hired as a teacher.
My husband started looking for another job, but couldn't find one. The

*threats continued. My daughter was born in 2005 and I was worried
our life was going to be worse.*

Baghdad was just a place for dead bodies.

*We couldn't go to stores. One minute everything's okay, and then
the whole place is bombed and people are dying. The people that we
shopped from, our friends, they would disappear. Death started to be
normal. I don't want to say this but it was not shocking us to know
that 500 died in the shopping center or there's this car with a bomb
here in this street or that street and how close it was to us. Iraqis started
to adjust to these situations.*

*But then one night a big eighteen-wheeler truck carrying a huge
bomb came to the place where my husband worked. The target was
the Americans. They were very close to the gate when it exploded. I
had been sleeping but the explosion shook the windows in my room,
the noise unimaginable.*

For part of one agonizing day, Asinja did not know whether her husband was dead or alive after the bomb, which killed many of his friends.
She waited for news. Finally she learned that Saher was alive, but they
knew they had to flee Iraq if they were to survive. However, Asinja and
the children did not have passports. Saher had a passport, so he went, leaving Asinja and the kids behind. Every day was a struggle for Asinja, who
did her best to protect her children and give them a sense of security and
love while waiting for word from Saher.

In Ankara, Saher learned about international law protecting refugees.
He qualified because he was Yazidi fleeing genocide in Iraq. However, a
file for refugee status could not be opened until Asinja and his children
were with him. He received a temporary visa to remain in Turkey and
landed a job working illegally in a clothing factory, making half of what a
Turkish citizen earned.

The real nightmare now began for Asinja.

Getting Out Alive

With the help of family and friends and my salary, we gave money to my brother-in-law to get passports for us. They were full of mistakes, like our names were spelled wrong, the dates of birth were wrong. But we could use them. Iraq is not like here. Now, the challenge started, how to get to the airport. My husband's friend who worked at the Baghdad International Airport booked a flight for us for the middle of August.

We prepared, got the luggage and got my kids prepared and said goodbye, crying. We left in the car with the same friend of my husband who worked in the airport. I put the kids in the back of the car and I sat in front. He drove a little bit and then he told me, "I have to tell you something, the road is very dangerous. We might be attacked. Try to stay calm and when I say lie down, get down." My eyes filled with tears.

I was already sad because I left Baghdad. I hadn't had a chance to say goodbye to my parents. So I just looked back at my kids, and I held their hands. I thought, I'm putting my kids in this situation, but I cannot go back. I was so frightened and confused. I was seeing death very close.

I was scared for my kids, so I told them we're going to play a game. It's a game called hiding. I said, "When I say hide, we all go down in the car and hide ourselves on the floor, and when I say that's it, we can just get back up." They laughed, and we began to play.

But the driver started to sweat, his skin so pale, and he said, "Asinja, they're here," and suddenly there was shooting from everywhere. Cars were in front of us and behind and there was nowhere to go.

"Now!" I said to my kids. And we got all down. Even the driver, who was holding the steering wheel, was also hiding. I was thinking, If we're not going to get killed with their guns, we will get killed in a car

accident. My daughter was so scared of the sound of the bullets, she started to cry. My son was trying to hold it together. "No," he told her, "this is a game we are playing."

But the driver knew we couldn't make it. When he had the opportunity he turned around because even if we got through this, he said, on the road ahead there were more. He took us back to our home.

We missed the flight, and I called my husband. He said, "We have to find a way," so he talked to his friend about the best day and time to leave. So we tried it again, we got new tickets, we headed to the airport and the same scenario happened. Again.

We went back, but I was not emptying my bags. There had to be a way. The driver came back to my house, and told of his plan to take us very early in the morning. My husband's family was warning us against it. "You'll be a clear target. You'll be the only car in the street." But the driver was sure. He issued another set of tickets and picked us up at 4:00 A.M. And that time, we passed safely. There was no attack. I could not have been more grateful to my husband's friend.

But I was very sad to leave Iraq. I was worried about the future in Istanbul. I didn't even get excited about seeing my husband because my worries and fears were so big. Bigger than me.

Once inside the small terminal, Asinja cried uncontrollably. Sad about fleeing Iraq and facing an uncertain future in Turkey, Asinja was leaving her family and friends behind. She had loved Baghdad from the moment she moved there. It represented hope. Yet the city she loved had been transformed into something ugly.

A New Word, a New World

As we landed on September 15, 2007, I could see Istanbul. There were orange buildings and the sea, and as the plane lowered I could see people walking on the shore. There were ships and boats and I loved that, those things that made it so different from Iraq. And one thing I

noticed, the sky was so clear. There was no dust like in Iraq. The sky
was blue and the view was like the pictures we had seen on calendars
of places we thought we'd never go.

My husband met us at the airport with a taxi. On the drive to
his apartment I noticed that even the smell of the streets was differ-
ent. They say because of the bombs and the war after war, the
weather in Iraq and the environment is not clear. Now I knew what
they meant.

After the ecstasy of the moment, the reality of the challenges ahead took
root. Following protocol, they registered with the United Nations High
Commissioner on Refugees. Their file was expedited as they were the only
Yazidi family in Istanbul. Over the past few months, two Yazidi villages
near her home village had been attacked and many people were killed.

A U.N. official explained that Asinja and her family qualified as
refugees—a word that Asinja had never heard before.

I never thought that I would be a refugee. I thought I would travel just
to see the world like the girls I saw in the movies. Maybe I'd get a schol-
arship studying at a university. My dreams were so big that I was
thinking about Harvard. But to enter as a refugee, instead, I didn't
understand what I was being told. I'd been discriminated against
because of my religion and thought maybe this was yet another way
to label me a Yazidi. So I asked about going to Australia or Germany
where there were many Yazidi families. The man said the United States
might work since my husband had had a job with Americans. I didn't
let myself get too excited, as I had been disappointed before.

They spent months in Istanbul. Asinja did not speak Turkish or know
where to go to complete even the most basic tasks. She also did not know
what to do with their children. In their apartment, she sat near a window,
wishing she might hear Arabic. Her husband worked long hours. Asinja
felt isolated and depressed.

*But one day, as I cooked lunch for the kids, through the open window
I heard people speaking Arabic. They were a Christian couple with a
baby girl, and they had just arrived from Baghdad, who rented the
apartment under ours.*

*Soon after, as I was shopping, I met a family from Bashiqa, and
we became friends. They treated me like their daughter.*

*Still, the nine months we waited was the longest in my life,
though it was considered a fast case there. We met with the International Catholic Migration Commission. To obtain refugee status we needed to get medical checkups and a security check. Then
we waited. There was no timetable. You just wait until they contact you.*

Finally, Asinja and her family were given a travel date to the United
States for May 25, 2008. But then their trip was canceled. According to
their official documentation, they were supposed to be living in the Turkish city of Tokat, and it was discovered that they had stayed in Istanbul.
Clearly, they had not paid the right bribe to the right official.

Saher had to quit his job, they had to move out of their apartment, and
after a thirteen-hour bus ride to Tokat they immediately registered and paid
the Turkish "tax" required to leave the country. After some time in Tokat,
they returned to Istanbul with no apartment or job awaiting them, so they
stayed with a Syrian family that was also waiting for a flight. Finally,
another call: their departure date would be June 25, 2008, nearly a year
after Asinja had arrived in Turkey.

*We went to a culture orientation meeting and they asked us if we knew
someone in the United States. So I told them we didn't. They told us
that if you know someone, we can take you to that place, but if you
don't know, we're going to pick the place for you. So they picked Houston. We asked, "Where is Houston?" They said, "Houston is in Texas,
a state in the south."*

Our Iraqi friends made fun of us. "Oh, you're going to live with horses and cows. We see you having these big hats and you will be like cowboys."

Then my husband said, "Anywhere is better than Baghdad, and it's better than Istanbul. I just want to be stable. It's been years. We are on our way."

So I was ready. I called my parents. I remember joking with my dad, "You know what? I will see Tom Cruise very soon." He said, "You will be successful and you will be happy. Your life is going to change. The things that we could not give to you when you were in Bashiqa, you will have for sure."

On their departure day, the International Organization of Migration gave them a sealed envelope with all their papers and strict instructions not to open it. At the airport they remained terrified. It was only after they crossed the red line at passport control and showed their papers did they finally feel relief.

While at the airport, Asinja met a group of American women traveling together. They were welcoming and engaged her in conversation over coffee.

They were so friendly, they accepted us, and they really didn't care about what we believed, what's our color, where we're from. And when I saw that they are women who travel together once a year without their husbands and have fun, I realized that could be my life and my daughter's life. As a woman in the U.S. one has choice and freedom.

From Istanbul they flew to Frankfurt, Germany, and then to New York City.

As we were landing in New York, the pilot started to do a tour. We saw the freedom statue. I couldn't believe that I was seeing it because it seemed so far when I was in Bashiqa. You know, when you dream of a place a lot, you just feel like it's in your imagination, it doesn't really exist because it's so far, it's so impossible to see. Now it became a symbol of my happiness, actually. My freedom. I looked at it really as an opportunity for magic.

They finally arrived at their new home in Houston, where they were being resettled. Representatives from Interfaith Ministries of Greater Houston took them to a one-bedroom apartment. On June 26, 2008, a new life began for Asinja and her family.

Making a Life

Our apartment had tables, chairs, a bed and blankets for us, for each of my kids. There was a lot of food in the kitchen, pots, everything we needed was there for us. We were on the second floor facing the pool. It was such a beautiful view.

It did not take the couple long to meet other refugees from Iraq and learn how to navigate a new world. Like all refugees they had I-94 status, which allowed them to work and apply for a social security number. Only upon receipt of the number could they apply for official ID cards. Asinja got her Green Card in 2009, after a year in America. She soon enrolled in an English course, where she had been accepted at the highest level. Her husband was in the most basic level. They each went for four hours a day so they could take turns with the kids.

One day a visitor came from the local church. Her name was Anne and she said she was just a church member trying to find refugees to listen to them, to help them. I told her about my journey, and we cried together. And she hugged me, she prayed for me. And I told her the part that was really hurting me because I didn't have a chance to say goodbye to my parents because of the war. So she said if you allow me, I will be your mom or your grandma here.

Anne taught Asinja about the public bus system, the schools, and the community colleges where Asinja might be able to start her studies. It was not easy learning how to navigate American bureaucracy and paperwork. But with Anne as her guide, Asinja was an outstanding student.

She took the proficiency exam at the local community college, where she flourished in English but needed to take three remedial math classes. While other refugees received financial aid, Asinja was told she was not eligible. Asinja remained tenacious and resilient. Anne told her about a course in first aid and CPR training, and that there was a need for people with such a background. Asinja and Saher got jobs, but there was so much yet to do and figure out: enrolling the children in school, getting a driver's license, preparing a résumé, and getting into community college.

After several months, Asinja enrolled in Samuel Houston Community College, where financial aid officials told her she was fully qualified. So, after many years of waiting, she finally resumed her studies and entered community college in 2009. She was working full time, taking care of her children, and excelling in school. She quickly moved from two to five classes a semester and accomplished her goal of straight As. One of the greatest days of her life was when she received her associate's degree in 2012.

> *Through these years, I was helping every refugee who I met. I told Interfaith that I wanted to do the same thing they did for me, and help as much as I can. So I volunteered with Interfaith Ministries Alliance, Catholic Charities, YMCA, translating, interpreting, doing food stamp application, taking people to social security offices, teaching new refugees. When you have dreams and goals inside you for a long time, it really becomes like a fuel that is hidden for the right opportunity. And once this opportunity comes, then you can distribute this fuel all around yourself to others.*

In the spring of 2013 she started part-time studies at the University of Houston, where she had a scholarship to pursue petroleum engineering.

However, in early August 2014 the plight of the Yazidi people became known to the world. Terrifying pictures of 50,000 Yazidis trapped by ISIS on Mount Sinjar dominated the news. Fortunately, her parents and most of the villagers had managed to flee before the devastation.

> *They burned our house, burned all the trees, destroyed all of Bashiqa. I don't know how a person, a human, can do all this. My family didn't take anything with them. Hearing their stories, I knew we had to raise the awareness. So I chose to leave college and fight for my people. We started fund-raising, raising awareness.*

Asinja returned to Iraq in early 2015. She sat with the victims and listened to their painful stories. Except for her brother, who had come to Houston with his wife, her entire family was in an Iraqi refugee camp. The years of violence had taken a toll on her parents, who were both ill. She saw friends who had lived so peacefully in Bashiqa, now victims of terror that had torn their lives apart.

In 2014, an international organization called Yazda was formed to bring attention to the plight of the Yazidis and Christian minorities in Iraq. During her visit Asinja went to the Yazda Center in Dohuk, in Iraqi Kurdistan, to hear stories of the women and girls raped by Islamic State members. Asinja comforted the victims as she had been one of them. The trip was profoundly painful. But it also helped Asinja realize that her life's calling was to help the most vulnerable on earth—persecuted minorities and refugees. She wrote several articles and upon her return to Houston, changed her major to business administration to acquire the skills needed for organizational work. She graduated in 2017 and is now pursuing an MBA with a focus on leadership at Houston University. Asinja works as operations manager at a Houston investment company. She has also taught Arabic in the public schools, for which she was recognized by the mayor of Houston.

Asinja met the most noted spokesperson for the plight of the Yazidis, Nadia Murad, when she was in Houston, and they formed a deep bond.

She had been held captive for three years and was tortured and raped before managing to escape. She had spoken to the U.N. and was appointed the first goodwill ambassador for the dignity of survivors of human trafficking for the United Nations. Nadia was awarded the Nobel Peace Prize in 2018. Asinja later traveled with Nadia to Germany to help translate and work with her as Nadia finished her memoir, *The Last Girl*. Asinja also went to England with her to meet with her attorney, Amal Clooney, and was thrilled to get to meet Amal's husband, George. Asinja's relationship with Nadia has been very important in shaping her work to educate people about the Yazidis, their traditions, and the genocide they suffered.

Asinja and her husband now own their own home in Houston. Their children are flourishing in public school.

> *I put them into this environment that I was always dreaming of, seeing my children have opportunities, doing well at school, having fun, and participating. My daughter sings a lot in the choir and they invited her to sing the national anthem. And my son is playing a cello. I'm glad I made the decision to get into that taxi again on that road in the middle of the night.*
>
> *I am proud to be an American. But I will never stop dreaming and remembering my village, my mother and my neighborhood friends. When I walk in Houston in the fall, I smell Bashiqa and feel overflowing pride knowing that I'm setting a strong example of determination and inspiration for Yazidi women everywhere.*

CHAPTER 4

DENG AJAK JONGKUCH

SOUTH SUDAN

*There were thousands of us walking. Walking day and night. I had
nothing in my mind except survival for one more day. You see friends
being shot or dying from disease. All we could do was keep going, trying to get a little food and water and hope that we would escape being
attacked by militias. That was my life for a year.*

Deng Ajak Jongkuch survived an unimaginable journey from one refugee camp to another in Sudan, walking about 1,000 miles for over a year,
separated from his parents, sleeping in the jungle, not knowing whether
he would live another day.

This region became well known to the world through the plight of Deng
and all the other "Lost Boys" in the 1990s as well as the plight of the people
of Darfur (another region of Sudan) in the first decade of the twenty-first
century. Sudan has been rooted in conflict since its independence in 1956
from the Anglo-Egyptian co-rule. It is an oil-rich country. However, ethnic, religious, political, and tribal conflicts have dominated the area since
independence.

National politics were controlled by military regimes favoring Islamic-
oriented governments that spurred two civil wars over the course of the
twentieth century. Such conflicts were rooted in "northern economic,
political and social domination of largely non-Muslim, non-Arab southern Sudanese." The first civil war, triggered by the southern Sudanese Anya
Nya insurgency movement, began in 1955 and ended in 1972 with over a
half million people dying. The Addis Ababa peace agreement between the
government and the Southern Sudan Liberation Movement provided some
stability to the region for about a decade.

This peace did not last. A second civil war was sparked in 1983 when
the military regime attempted to implement Sharia law "as part of its overall policy to 'Islamize' all of Sudan." The war ravaged the region, with
over 2 million people dying from the war, disease, and starvation over a
period of twenty-two years.

It was not until 2005 that the North/South Comprehensive Peace Agree-ment "granted the southern rebels autonomy for six years followed by a referendum on independence for Southern Sudan." This referendum was held in January 2011, and on July 9, 2011, South Sudan became an inde-pendent nation.

The Second Sudanese Civil War sparked one of the most notorious child migrations, whose population came to be known as the Lost Boys of Sudan. Over 33,000 children, mostly Dinka boys between the ages of seven and seventeen, were separated from their families. They trekked enormous dis-tances through the wilderness, seeking refuge from the fighting. They crossed Sudan into Ethiopia and back, with many dying along the way. The survivors are now in camps in Kenya, Sudan, and Uganda. About 3,800 were relocated to the United States.

Since December 2013, civil war has ravaged South Sudan, and, accord-ing to the United Nations High Commissioner for Refugees (UNHCR), more than 2.5 million people have been forced to leave the country and seek safety, while nearly 2 million people have been internally displaced.

An estimated 330,000 people have died since independence in 2011 in what is now the third civil war in the region. Amid the turmoil, there remains some hope. If peace were to be attained, the oil could create resources to support both South Sudan and Sudan. Although the conflict is increasing, Deng, now an American citizen and fully committed to his life here, holds on to hope for his country of birth.

For my country to survive and flourish, we need more education. That is why through the nonprofit Impact a Village we have built a school in Malek, South Sudan where over 600 students are currently studying. Each time I go there and see the students, I leave with the feeling that perhaps Sudan's future can be brighter than its past.

He Threw Garbage on Me

I was born in South Sudan in a village called Kolnyang. Actually I don't know my birthday. I don't know the month, I don't even know my age. I could be forty, I could be eighty. But what I do know and what all refugees need to understand, is that it's true what you hear about the United States. It is a country of milk and honey. But you need to climb to get the honey. You need to work hard to get the milk.

A Childhood of War

Deng was the firstborn of nine children. His mother, Amour, and father, Ajak, were members of the Dinka (Jieng) tribe, the largest tribe in present-day South Sudan. Deng was raised in a *tukul*, a hut made of dried grass with a thatched roof, mud walls, and a dirt floor. The village lacked electricity and had only one well.

When he was about three, he went, as people there do to this day, to a cattle camp that his family and many relatives owned. There he spent about five years with cow's milk as his only nourishment.

I went straight from my mother's milk to cow's milk and that sustained me throughout my childhood. If a cow dies, then you get to eat the meat.

The boys and girls took care of the cattle and went out to graze them during the day. He and the other children were taken care of by his uncle. He saw his parents only once a year when the cows would graze out toward his home village. There was no school at the camp, so his days were spent working and playing with the other children. In a world with no toys or any real material possessions they had to invent their own. The boys wrestled, and they enacted mock weddings. They made cows out of mud, then negotiated the number of cows for the bride they wanted. Years later, the game would become reality—after much negotiation, Deng paid seventy cows and goats as a dowry to wed his wife.

And then the war between Northern and Southern Sudan started in 1983, and by 1987 it had become so intense that the government forces started attacking the villages, looking for the rebels. One night, our village was burned, many were killed, and we fled. The soldiers told us that the safest place for us to go was a refugee camp. My parents, who were back at home, didn't come with me. I went by myself, with two cousins, and other boys, some girls and families.

That's how I ended up in Parnyidu Refugee Camp in Ethiopia in 1987. We walked from Bor, the area where our village was, to Ethiopia. It took us about three weeks. We walked every single day. I had no shirt, no shoes. At night, we slept in the jungle, worried we might be attacked by the Sudanese military. There were thousands, thousands of people. We met other people on the way and the number became huge. You don't even know who was walking with you. But my cousins and I stayed together along the way. A lot of people died on the way because of starvation, lack of clean drinking water, of malaria.

Deng always kept the words his parents said to him when he left for the cattle camp close to his heart. "Never give up hope, Deng, no matter what happens."

We stayed in Parnyidu for about four years. Initially, nobody came to help us. There were thousands of us there. But we received no humanitarian aid for a couple of months because, what I learned later, the humanitarian people thought that we were not refugees.

The United Nations thought they were child soldiers and thus did not qualify for assistance. While the United Nations officials spent weeks debating the issue of their status, there were outbreaks of cholera, measles, and chicken pox in the camp.

Deng was one of about 30,000 children who had no parents with them. The children were dying from starvation and disease. After months went by, the U.N. started delivering food and blankets. Some children were dying of despair; others tried to return to their village but were killed along the way. Many, like Deng, built their own mud structures and made flour by pounding the grain they were given.

More months passed before the United Nations opened schools at the camp in 1988.

> *I had never been to school. We built our own classroom out of mud with a thatched roof and the teachers were anyone who had gone to school at all. They started teaching us the alphabet. We wrote letters with sticks on the dirt floor. There were no books. I went to the third grade.*

The world that Deng knew for four years ended abruptly in 1991 when a new Ethiopian government expelled thousands of refugees. The humanitarian agencies left when the situation grew increasingly dangerous. For Deng, another, more difficult chapter was about to unfold.

He and the other children fled the camp and swam across the crocodile-filled Gilo River. Many did not know how to swim and drowned. But Deng and the rest of the boys crossed the river and fled across the border to a town in Sudan. They found safety at Pacholla, a camp under the control of the rebel forces (Sudan People's Liberation Army).

Surviving the Camps

> *Once again, thousands of children had nothing: no food, no shelter, no peace. We survived on wild fruits, vegetables and by hunting animals. But so many people were dying of malnutrition, starvation, disease, no medicine. We had nothing.*

Deng was perhaps eleven or twelve at this point. He recalls the bombs falling from the sky from the Russian Antonov planes. But then one night they heard the roar of the planes, and instead of bombs, it was the International Red Cross, which, unable to land, was dropping sacks of beans and corn grains.

Four months later, Sudan Armed Forces penetrated the camp through Ethiopia. They crossed the water with their tanks and other big equipment. Again, life changed for Deng. Pacholla was attacked, and the children fled into the jungle. Despite the chaos, they followed others and ended up on the path to Kenya. Once again, Deng was on the run, into the unknown. This began the longest walk of his life, a journey of about 1,000 miles that lasted more than a year.

There was nothing in your mind except, How can I survive today? You're not even thinking about, why this is happening, why today, why me? All you can think about is food, water, not getting shot. You see your friends dropping and dying, being shot and some committing suicide as they could no longer bear the walking, the starvation, the unknown. There was no end in sight. All that I could think about was to keep walking. Otherwise I die.

Eventually, Deng and 16,000 children and teens arrived in Kakuma in 1992 (14,000 had died or fled on the long journey to Kenya). This was the beginning of the refugee camp, and again, no food, shelter, or services awaited them. (Today Kakuma is the largest refugee camp in sub-Saharan Africa with nearly 200,000 refugees.) For the first time in his life Deng was given a refugee card. After several months, they started getting food and medicine from the UNHCR. Generally, there was enough food for one meal a day. A school was started with minimal supplies and books, with one book for about twenty-five students.

Deng spent nearly nine years in Kakuma. While there, his life became the most stable it had been since his days at the cattle camp. In 1997 at Kakuma Refugee Camp, Deng met Yar, who would later become his wife. With few girls at the camp there was lots of competition to befriend one. Yar had made an incredible journey of her own. She left her village in 1988 to seek safety in Ethiopia with her aunt. Deng and Yar started spending more time together, but always in her aunt's tent and usually with others around. It was not in their culture to take a walk or sit together outside.

Though Yar had a lot of young men interested in her, she and Deng grew very fond of each other and fell in love.

In 1998, the plight of the Lost Boys became known in the United States. Their compelling story ignited compassion in most people who heard about the children who had walked thousands of miles on their own, surviving against all odds.

Under the leadership of President Bill Clinton that year, the United States got involved in the plight of the Lost Boys. However, the rules were clear about the issuance of immigration visas: they were only for unaccompanied children who were not married and who didn't have parents, who had previously been in a refugee camp in Ethiopia (meaning those who had walked the thousand miles to Kakuma), and who had registered with the UNHCR. These criteria applied to nearly all 16,000 of the Lost Boys at Kakuma Refugee Camp.

In my first interview with a U.S. official, he wanted to establish my identity, that I was a refugee, the reasons I left Sudan, my age, that I was single and whether my parents were with me. That's when they assigned my birth date of January 1, 1981, the same date assigned to most Lost Boys.

After three years and seven lengthy interviews, Deng received a letter that started with five precious words: "Welcome to the United States." Deng was one of 3,800 who received this letter. Most did not. Deng was told to sign many papers, which he did not comprehend, including one stating that he owed the government $800 for the cost of the plane ticket to the United States. Finally, he received his departure date. Yar was pregnant but could not go with him. He later learned that he was the father of a baby girl, Anyieth, and sent Yar money to rent an apartment in Nairobi, Kenya.

Acclimating to America

It was March 2001. I waited with ninety others to fly from Nairobi to America. This was my first time on an airplane. Everybody was white except us. We didn't know if they were Latinos or Russian or Chinese. I went to the bathroom and pressed some knob and it disappeared. What happened? Where did it go? None of us could believe it. They gave us food, but I had never seen a fork or knife before, so I ate with my hands. We had to stop in Amsterdam, and our guide from Immigration took us to a restaurant and spaghetti was served to everyone. I just came from a refugee camp. Is this real food? I wondered.

After more layovers three other guys and I arrived in San Jose, California. We were in a van and every few minutes, it kept stopping. None of us understood why. Finally, we asked what was going on and we were told what traffic lights are, with red meaning stop and green meaning go. This we just could not believe. Who was controlling this? I had never been around electricity in my life.

That night in March 2001 began the next chapter in Deng's journey. The following months would be devoted to learning about American culture: pizza, running water, cars, apartments, and how to interview for a job. He was told, "Be sure to always smile."

After a while, Deng was reminded of the $800 debt for his flight. For three months, he received Medicaid, food stamps, and a cash allowance for rent. After that, he had to support himself.

I got a job as a stock person at Pottery Barn Kids. It was very difficult. My English was not that good at the time. I was in the stock room and they would speak to me over a walkie-talkie so communication was not good. They knew that I'm good at putting things together and cleaning them, but finding things in the store, I had no idea. Everything was new. Everything was strange. Picture, prints, baby bumper, quilt, red gingham, Sabrina basket liner, vinyl. I was trying my best, but I was failing.

The manager, Sarah Long, called me into her office. She asked what was wrong. I explained about my background as a Lost Boy and that I had never seen the things they sold in the store. She listened to me.

She understood me. But the company said that Sarah had to reduce my hours and I could no longer receive benefits. I was earning minimum wage salary of nine dollars an hour, and with my roommate, we managed to pay the rent and barely had enough money for one simple meal a day. Gradually, by working hard, studying the store catalog and asking for help from others, I returned to full-time status. I made a wonderful friend at the store named Stephanie and she invited me to her parents' home in southern California. They took me to Disneyland. I thought that the crocodiles and snakes on the jungle ride were real.

Sarah made a major difference in my life and I would like to again thank her. I don't know where she is right now. I wish I could see her and communicate with her again. I tried to Google her name, but I learned that Sarah Long is a pretty common name. It is important for people to take the time to listen to the plight of refugees. Everyone wishes to be heard. And we need support to adjust to our new lives.

Deng survived an unimaginable journey from one refugee camp to another in Sudan, walking for over a year (about 1,000 miles), separated from his parents, sleeping in the jungle, not knowing if he would be killed. But the lowest point of his life came in July 2001 in America. While Deng was walking home in San Jose, California, a man stopped and offered him a ride. When Deng politely declined, the man took out a large garbage bag filled with rotten banana peels, spoiled milk, coffee grounds, and cigarette butts and threw it on him.

This was the lowest time in my life. It was worse than people trying to kill me in South Sudan. This hurt more as it impacted my soul. I didn't know whether it was my color or that I did not speak English well or whatever. I just wanted to leave and go back to the refugee camp. Nobody had ever thrown garbage on me. I was sitting there smelling all the garbage that covered me. I went to my apartment crying. I locked myself in my room and thought I should return to a refugee camp.

I couldn't sleep that night. At about 4 A.M., I was thinking over and over, why would this person do this to me? Is it the color of my skin? Is it because I'm tall? Is it because the clothes I wear or is it because I talk with different accent? I couldn't comprehend why he did this to me.

Then I realized that it wasn't about me. It's about how they see me. It's them. It's not me. I didn't do anything for this guy to throw garbage on me. I didn't do anything for Sarah to like me for who I am. It's how they see me. So, then I realized, okay, if it is them, how they see me, then I shouldn't take this one seriously. Why should I even think of going back to a refugee camp? People are going to see you differently anyway according to what they perceive to be true of you.

In 2004, Deng quit his job at Pottery Barn to work the night shift as a security guard while attending De Anza Community College. He worked from midnight to 8:00 A.M., then took the train home, showered, and slept for a few hours until going to school in the late morning. From then until 9:00 P.M., he was in class and studying. Then off to work again. Day after day.

After graduating in 2006, and having saved some money, he decided he was ready to apply to be a U.S. citizen so that he could bring Yar and his daughter to the States. But he was told that the U.S. immigration office had lost his file. Despite the fact that he had copies of everything, his case was stalled in a bureaucratic quagmire for years.

Finding Family, Forging Friendships

During that time, Deng yearned to see Yar and meet his daughter, who was already five years old. He wanted to visit the village that he had left eighteen years earlier. He wanted to know if his parents were still alive. So, with money he had saved, he returned to South Sudan. After a long flight in a U.N. cargo plane, he ended up in a village that was many miles from Kolnyang. After nine hours of walking, after so many years and so many nightmares, he entered his home village, excited and nervous.

I introduced myself to the villagers and asked the way to my parent's hut. Now there were two huts, one of which I learned had been built for my brothers and sisters. A lot of people were there. It was a big social gathering. I thought, Whoa, why are there so many people here? They didn't know I was coming. Then a woman who I knew was my mom came over and said, "Who's that?" And all the people surrounded us. I explained myself several times. And my mom didn't believe me. It was dark and she couldn't see my face. Besides, I was older, well fed, was wearing nice clothes. It had been eighteen years. I hardly recognized her too, but I knew it was my mom.

Then she ran, grabbed the dry grass and lit a fire so that she could see my face. She held the fire up and tried to recognize me. And then she said, "If you are my son, what is the nickname that I gave you when you were a kid?" And I told her, "My nickname was Makuol." And then she broke down. She cried. We hugged. And everybody was celebrating.

And then my dad came, and my uncle, and I felt so excited. So I asked, "Where's my grandma?" And they said, "Your grandma just died yesterday." I was so sad. I missed my grandma by one day. But the good thing was that I was at her funeral.

The village, scarred by decades of war and violence, still had no water or electricity. Deng spent two weeks there, getting to know his siblings. He saw children learning the alphabet in the dirt the same way he had. He realized he had to go back to America and tell his story. People needed to know what had happened, all the suffering, and what was still going on. Telling that story would become his mission in life.

In 2008, Deng met two remarkable humanitarian philanthropists, Lisa Frankel Wade and Cara France, who took an immediate liking to him. Together they formed the nonprofit Impact a Village, which seeks to improve education in poor villages throughout the world. Their first goal was to build a school in South Sudan and highlight awareness about the lessons of Deng's story. He even co-wrote with Lisa a beautiful children's book about his life, "A Story of Hope."

Despite working full time at their jobs and with Deng still in school, Deng and Lisa spoke together at many schools, churches, synagogues, mosques, and community centers. Deng felt it was his duty to help those in need. They raised enough money to fulfill Deng's dream of building a school in South Sudan. In 2010, Deng directed the building of the Malek Primary School in the Bor region. It now has 700 students, despite continued unrest in South Sudan.

After Deng told Cara and Lisa about his battles with immigration, they hired an attorney for him. Finally, in 2010, two days after the attorney filed a lawsuit, he was given an apology. A few days later, on April 23, 2010, he was sworn in as a U.S. citizen.

One Man's Commitment to Lifting Others

For Deng, education was the key to shaping a better future. Deng continued his studies at San Jose State University with a major in health services and administration. After graduating in 2008, he entered Touro University to earn a master's degree in public health in 2011. During all his years of studying he worked full time. His wife and children continued to live in Kenya; he sent them money each month and visited at least once a year.

After graduating, he returned to South Sudan for two years, working with Partners in Compassionate Care, a nonprofit that helps people in the country's rural villages. He managed its hospitals and clinics in the Bor region. This was an exciting time in South Sudan. It had become an independent country on July 9, 2011, and people were filled with hope. No one anticipated it would implode into the chaos and violence that exists today.

Deng kept trying to get his wife and four children entry visas to the States. However, the vetting process was long and thorough. At times he was about to give up hope, but that is not in his nature. Finally, in 2013, his family was reunited in Grand Rapids, Michigan, where they live today. They now have five children, ranging in age from three to sixteen. The couple just purchased their first house after three years of saving, driving for Uber and Lyft, and Yar working seven days a week in a car parts manufacturing company.

Deng is a hardworking, compassionate, personable, and outgoing man. He wants his children to get the best education. Deng's internal stability has guided him through a life of total uncertainty.

Deng runs Partners in Compassionate Care, which built a hospital about thirty miles north of his village and supports three rural clinics. He directs the hospital and clinics from Michigan and visits South Sudan often. He also makes time to speak at schools to keep his story and message alive. He is now raising funds for a Sudanese Community Center in Grand Rapids that will provide social services for refugees, including literacy training, financial planning, health and nutrition education, and preparation for citizenship, as well as a variety of cultural activities. He is deeply committed to helping refugees obtain the skills to succeed in America.

The most important thing for me is to share my story. It helps me to get out of my trauma that I went through. There is too much hurt inside of me, I need people to learn from my experience. I don't want anyone to ever suffer like this.

One does not feel his nightmare when Deng speaks to schoolchildren. Rather, he conveys lessons in resilience, perspective, and hope. He tells them about his efforts to build a school in South Sudan, a country with a 90 percent illiteracy rate. He explains to the children that they should never give up on their beliefs of what they can do in life.

Deng wants his story known—not for pity for all that he suffered or applause for his courage—so that people can learn from it and appreciate what really matters in life.

I want to let them know that refugees are human, like any other human being. It just happens that this person is called a refugee, there's

a reason that he became a refugee. It is not his own making to be a
refugee. I want people to be open to everybody, regardless of race, reli-
gion, gender or where that person came from. I want people to show
the good part of their country, show the good part of their neighbor-
hood, show the good part of themselves as human beings—show all
this to new people you meet in school, at work, in life. Show the good
part of you as a human being.

After a childhood running from violence and war, Deng is still running.
However, he is now running toward something. He is running to keep his
family secure, to tell his story to as many people as possible so they can
learn important life lessons, and to help rebuild his war-torn country of
South Sudan. Deng is one of the 3,800 Lost Boys who came to America. But
Deng is no longer a boy nor is he lost. He is enriching the fabric of American life each day with his story, his optimism, and his commitment.

CHAPTER 5

SIDONIA LAX

POLAND

As the saying goes, yesterday is history. Tomorrow is a mystery. And
today is a gift. I truly believe it. Today is a gift, a life. All I want to do
with this gift is to tell the next generation to be strong, to read and
learn, so that this should never happen again to anybody. People don't
call me a survivor. They call me a thriver.

Sidonia Lax was one of the many Polish Jewish children who saw a stable
and good life from her birth in 1927 completely dismantled with the Nazi
invasion in 1939. She has fond memories of her childhood and the perseverance and positive attitude that she was given by her mother that would
last a lifetime.

Little did Sidonia's mother know that these skills and work ethic would
later save her daughter's life. Poland's precarious location between Nazi-
controlled Germany and the Soviet Union during World War II had profound implications for the country and its people. Both Germany and the
Soviet Union invaded Poland, which saw hundreds of thousands of casu-
alties and deaths as the country was divided into two occupied territo-
ries. However, the worst was still to come for the millions of Poles who
remained. Polish resistance to the occupation was fierce, but the resistance often led to entire towns being massacred as retaliation by SS death
squads.

The Nazis did not want Germany to be their killing fields, so they
chose to put many of their death camps in Poland, with Auschwitz the
most infamous. It is estimated that at least 1.6 million non-Jewish Polish
civilians and 3 million Jewish citizens of Poland, as well as millions of
others sent there on trains, were killed by the Nazis during World
War II. Approximately 1.5 million Poles were deported to forced-labor
camps.

Thousands of Poles willingly supported the deportation and extermination of Polish Jews. There are several theories why there was such fer-
vent anti-Semitism in some elements of Polish society, but Polish history

is known both for welcoming Jews and for its anti-Semitism. These theories are largely based on religious, economic, and historical understandings of the region, and as in Germany, Jews were largely blamed for a variety of Poland's problems. While such claims were, of course, false, they had a profound impact on the populace and the actions that befell many Jews in Poland.

Today, there is a prominent and well-visited Jewish museum in Warsaw, POLIN Museum of the History of Polish Jews. It highlights the many contributions made to Polish society by Jews throughout the ages. The remaining Jewish community struggles to survive in areas such as Warsaw and Krakow, where there are Jewish community centers and synagogues. In January 2018 a law was passed in Poland that made it illegal to suggest that Poland was complicit in the Holocaust in any way. Anyone found guilty of claiming that Poland played a role in the systematic mass murder of Jews in the Polish death camps could face a steep fine or up to three years in prison. The law was revised in July 2018 to reduce it to a civil offense. Much controversy continues to surround this policy.

Sidonia has many albums of pictures and letters in her home in Los Angeles. Looking through them, one can see her life story and can begin to understand the impact that this woman has had on others since 1991, when she started sharing her story. The telling of her journey uplifts her and inspires her to keep going. It is her lifeblood.

There is one letter out of the hundreds she still has that she wants to share with me. It was written in October 2000 by a high school student who had heard her speak. "Yesterday was truly a moment in my life I will never forget. Your energy and simple love of life was refreshing to hear and to see. I took away a positive feeling about myself as a person and my life. You made me see just how special life is and that we should never take it for granted. Your heartfelt words reached into my soul and showed me I should take advantage of the opportunities I have. To listen to you tell all of us to follow our hopes and dreams is something we all needed. You are a living role model."

The Apple Lady

The number one lesson is to learn how to cope no matter what life brings you. You cope with problems. You cope with death. You cope with killing. Learn to be tough, don't fall apart. It is a lesson that everybody should adapt in their own life every single day.

Born into Privilege, Raised for the Hardships of the Future

Born in June 1927 in Przemyśl, Poland, Sidonia was the only child of Isaac and Cyla Lewin.

Przemyśl was a rather midsized town in southern Poland in Galicia. Close to Carpathian Mountains. I had a governess who was with me all day long from the time I got up until I went to sleep. She watched me practice piano, and took me to ballet lessons. She took me skiing and skating, and to play with other children.

My mother was the go-getter, but both my parents ran the family business, an outerwear manufacturer.

We lived in a very small apartment. There was no running water, there were very rough wooden floors in the kitchen, a wooden-burning stove. But, we did have three housekeepers, one to cook, and two to perform all the other duties. The water had to be brought in, the wood had to be chopped, fire had to be started.

The thing that I remember very specifically, is my mother's ingenuity. She raised me for the future. Because, when I was about eight years old, I was taught everything there was to be done in a household. Everybody got a day off, and I had to scrub the floors with my little hands. I was crying but that didn't matter. The doors were locked, and I couldn't come out until it was finished.

I washed laundry on a scrub board, and boiled sheets on the stove. And then, I had to take it out, rinse it and hang it outside to dry. I was taught how to bake bread with yeast. How to wash, clean, sew,

*darn. All the socks had to be darned. I even had to learn how to darn
a damask tablecloth. And that was quite an art. But at that time, every
so-called lady of the house had to learn how to do it.*

*I was not allowed to ride a bicycle. Because it wasn't proper for a
lady to ride a bicycle. I was supposed to write. I played piano. Learned
literature and things like that.*

Sidonia grew up in an observant Jewish home where her parents followed the laws of Shabbat and celebrated all the Jewish holidays. She did
not want to learn Yiddish or Hebrew, and she resisted any attempt by her
parents to provide her with a religious education.

*In our city, they were two segments of the Jewish community: the
people that were very progressive and lived a modern life, and
the people that were insisting on living the way people lived a thousand years ago.*

*As far as I was concerned, I was a rebel. I went to public school, I
spoke Polish. I did not want to learn Yiddish or Hebrew.*

During the week she went to a public school, not a Jewish one where
many of her relatives attended. She does not recall experiencing any anti-
Semitism during those years. Her parents protected her from the news
coming out of Germany. She felt safe and had every reason to believe that
her life would continue as she knew it in Poland. Instilled in her from
childhood was the belief that Poland was a great country in which to live.

*I was not aware at all of anti-Semitism. Many, many of my friends
were Catholic. It's a Catholic country. But, I'm sorry to say, the minute the war broke out, those friends didn't know me anymore. I was
like a pariah, like a cancer, and they just abandoned me completely.*

Life in the Ghetto

Sidonia was only twelve years old when her world changed. It was 1939 and
Germany had invaded Poland. Her parents decided to flee, so they hired

a horse and wagon and journeyed toward the Romanian border. However, her parents decided to go back to gather more things.

> *Their possessions were important to them. Instead of running and getting out, because through Romania we could get to the United States, or go to South America, they made a very unwise decision to go back for a few more pillows and that was the end of it. They never came out alive.*

Her town was divided in half between the Germans and the Russians (who had by that time signed a nonaggression pact). Sidonia lived on the side of the San River under Russian authority.

> *I went to a Russian school. I wore a red handkerchief. Slowly, the Germans started organizing the Jews. It was so gradual that nobody could notice what was happening. First, the Jews weren't allowed to work in civil jobs. The professional people had to close their offices immediately. There were only very few places where one could earn a dollar. We were not allowed to walk on the street. We had to walk in the gutter, like slaves do.*
>
> *Gradually, we had to bring all our possessions to the police department. Like furs, jewelry, anything of any value. That was announced on the radio. We had no television. I was not allowed to go out at night and play with my friends. But I did have a radio. And I had to give up that radio which felt like half of my life was gone. It was like a prison.*
>
> *Then the Nazis came in. The first thing they did was create a ghetto. It had an electrified fence and barbed wire around it. The Jews were forced to wear yellow arm bands with Jewish stars. They gave me a job to smash big rocks with a sledge hammer into little tiny pebbles used for building new roads. That's important. Because I got amazing muscles, so large that I was ashamed of them. But they would help me later. We had to move to an apartment and share it with several*

other families. Ghetto was a life of misery. Very little food. Dead corpses on the street every day, either from malnutrition or from disease. Very few articles of hygiene. And the life was absolutely of idleness. When people have nothing to do, and have nothing to eat, people get in trouble.

A lot of the food was supplied by small children, who could squeeze underneath the fence of the ghetto, go outside and swap maybe a pair of shoes, or whatever one possessed, for a piece of bread, and bring it back for the family to eat. The big holiday was when one was rich enough to have a funeral. That meant that the wagon, which held the casket, would go out of the ghetto and come back filled with food.

Sometimes there was a knock at the door. "Pack your clothes. Take as much as you can carry. You're going to work." Big lie. They didn't go to work. They never came back.

So, slowly, very slowly, the people, the men in our apartment started digging a bunker. Under the building. Dirt, plain dirt. One area was higher to lie down in. The other area was deeper to stand in. In the corner was a big hole. This was our bathroom. Thirty people, all ages from babies to seniors, went into hiding in this bunker.

After a while, the hole, about twenty feet by thirty feet, was dug. The entrance was camouflaged by a couple of boards on hinges. When my parents felt it was getting more and more dangerous, thirty people went into that hole. People were coughing and sneezing and making noise, and little babies crying. There was not enough room for everybody to lie down. For everyone who did, another one had to stand up.

I was in this bunker for three long months. I didn't wash. I didn't change clothes. My skin became yellow like a lemon. My hair was full of lice. There was no sunshine. We didn't have anything to eat, so whoever could gather some food would bring it down. One day, they found only dry beans, which had to soak over twenty-four hours in order to cook. I was selected to hold the candle, to hold that candle until these beans got cooked. My finger was badly burned. Doctors had no medication, no drugs. So the doctors, all they could tell us was to eat a lot of raw onion and raw garlic. That develops immunity. I still have a scar.

My mother and others made a plan to escape, to hide with a Catholic family outside, and a Catholic policeman was supposed to look the other way. But when she went, he was not on duty. We heard shots. Slowly, slowly, people were disappearing from the ghetto and being killed outside.

At that time, I was eating from trashcan's leftovers. There I was, a teenager with no vitamins whatsoever for years now. My father had heard that somebody, somewhere, illegally, had some apples for sale. He wanted, in the worst way, to get an apple for me.

He never came back. And all I know is that I lost my father because of an apple. Every time I eat an apple, I remember him.

Here, Sidonia stops her story and weeps. For the memory of her cherished father, for her hope that people can value the "apples" in their lives while they have them. Today, she is known by thousands as "The Apple Lady" because of this story she tells, always with an apple in her hand.

Sidonia continues her story.

Now I was an orphan in this bunker with few people left. It didn't last very long. The Germans came with dogs and they snuffed us out. And we were discovered.

Sidonia and ten others were captured and taken to the jail in the ghetto. It was overseen by SS Unterscharfuheer Josef Schwemmbeger. One day looking out the window, Sidonia saw a family friend, Sala Friedman, who told her that both of her parents had been shot by Schwemmbeger. (After World War II, he hid in Argentina for forty years. He was arrested in 1991 and charged with the deaths of more than 3,400 Jews. He was found guilty of the mass execution in the Premyśl camp on September 2, 1943, and other crimes, and died in prison.) As it does for all survivors, luck played an important role in the journey of survival. Before her death, Sidonia's mother had pleaded with a policeman to save her daughter. He kept his promise and got her out of jail. As she left, she heard the gunshots killing the remaining people in the cell.

The Journey to Hell

So they put me on the train to Auschwitz. When we arrived, immediately they shaved our hair, took away the clothes that I had. I was given a sack, like a potato sack, with two holes cut out for arms and one for my head, no underwear and some kind of wooden shoes. They weren't really shoes. After two weeks, my hair had grown back a little bit, and they shaved a cross right onto my head.

I got my number, A-14821. Auschwitz was the only place where they gave tattoos.

Every morning, and it was December and there was a lot of ice, we had to line up and stand still for hours, like in the army, straight on our feet on the ice. If anybody hadn't relieved themselves in the bathroom early in the morning, they were killed right in front of us. We had to look at dead bodies every single day.

In the bunks, ten women slept in one upper bunk and ten women in one lower. There was one blanket. One blanket and if one wanted to turn, everybody woke up. Each day we were given a few minutes to wash, but it was impossible to do this with thousands of others trying to get the same access to the water and the toilets, but they insisted that people be clean.

The degradation was terrible, we were all profoundly depressed. We all knew the rules. Some decided to commit suicide by running up to the electric barbed wire. The punishment for that—one hundred others were immediately shot and killed. Every day there was what they called a selection, when SS men would come in and say, You go to the right and you go to the left. The people on the right disappeared. They were getting killed in crematoria. The people on the left stayed to work.

I was hungry. We were given one "meal" a day. It consisted of a piece of bread, cabbage soup that you could barely see a piece of cabbage floating around in and some coffee. That food had to last the entire day. So I learned how to make soles for the shoes. Sewed all the shoes of the people who worked in the kitchen and I got an extra bowl of soup. I was a shoemaker.

But I didn't stay very long, a few weeks maybe, before I was sent to the work camps. I knew it was because of my muscles and strength.

Working in Darkness

Her first work camp was Bergen-Belsen. Here Sidonia did hard labor for many hours a day, but she was given two or three meals some days, clothes, and her own bed.

The camps were in Germany. They were owned by German businesses or the government. They were located in a forest. So when we got a few minutes to go outside, they were full of animals, wild animals. But I wasn't afraid. We worked in the woods at night, so even today, I'm not afraid of darkness even though I know many things are happening.

I never gave up hope. All I was thinking about was having a full stomach and living until the next day. Nothing else. Just to survive a day. I was very fortunate to inherit my mother's and my grandmother's common sense. I had the muscles.

In late 1944, Sidonia was transported to Elsnig, a subcamp of Buchenwald. Her main job was in a factory, filling grenades with chemicals. She recalls the day that instead of filling the train with the grenades, they were forced onto the train to Berlin. She will never forget hearing the bombs dropping around them. The Allied forces believed that the trains were carrying ammunition, not people. The Nazi guards fled, and she and hundreds of others were on a train destined for death.

The train caught on fire. I was the first one to jump from the train.
My clothes were burning. I rolled on the ground, killed the fire, and
there we were, alive. We got some new clothes from farmers living
nearby. And we found a man who had a horse and buggy and two
other women and I convinced him to take us back to Poland.

I went back to Poland. And the cousin that I thought was killed,
the one we had sat Shiva for, greeted me at my family's door. They had
taken him into the Russian army. He had survived.

Adapting to a New Life

Soon after the war came to an end, many people Sidonia knew could not
cope with their newfound freedom. Many survived the nightmare and
then just collapsed, unable to recover. Sidonia credits her survival to all
that her mother taught her as a child, and it was that strength of body and
character that allowed her to go on, though she had to confront the reality that she was an orphan, that so many people she knew had died, and
that she had no home. She was filled with questions that she could not even
think about during the Holocaust.

Where was God? Why did it happen? How is it possible that little
children could be killed with bayonets? Why so much evil? How could
anyone commit these atrocities?

Indeed she was free, but she was entering a different world than the one
she had left behind six years earlier. She learned from her cousin that
except for him, an uncle in Los Angeles, and cousins now in Chicago, her
entire extended family had been killed. He explained to her that there was
no future in Poland and that they needed to leave. She joined him and
others on a journey where they were smuggled out, on foot, first to Czecho-
slovakia, then to Austria, and ultimately to Germany.

In Munich, she was declared a displaced person, as so many others were
after the war. These are people who have lost their families, their homes,

and their countries. The United States had strict immigration quotas and did not want people from Poland. Sidonia managed to get papers, declaring that she was German. While waiting for a visa to the United States, Sidonia managed to survive by working as a cook from 7:00 A.M. until 9:00 P.M. The living conditions were not much better than the work camps, but at least she was free and had realistic reasons to be hopeful.

Finally, in 1947, she was granted a visa, and HIAS (founded as the Hebrew Immigrant Aid Society; its name now is HIAS) helped her cross the sea for America.

First I arrived in New York, slept overnight in the HIAS office. We would be out in the middle of the night, and it seemed like everybody was awake. Nobody was sleeping. Everything was open. These were the good times in New York. I was there overnight, I went to Chicago by train, met my cousin.

It's amazing when I think about it today, the audacity, the nerve that I had at that time. I arrived in Chicago, I was supposed to look for my cousin and his wife, and they were going to hold a white handkerchief, but I couldn't find them. So, I called for a taxi. I had three dollars in my pocket, I had an address in my hand, and I arrived in their apartment.

They were beside themselves because they couldn't find me on the train station. Finally they arrived at their apartment and there I stood with my suitcase. They could not believe their eyes, that I found my way in a country without a language, with little money, without knowledge of anything of the habits of the country whatsoever. I was not afraid. I couldn't do it today, and it's amazing when you think about it.

I was there for one week and then I proceeded to California. There my uncle and my aunt had found for me some Polish friends so that I wouldn't feel lonely, and they had me registered in the local high school.

Finding Friendships, Love, and Purpose

Sidonia enrolled at Belmont High School, but she had a difficult time because of her limited English. Her uncle got her a job in a medical lab, saying that Sidonia had worked in one in Germany. Rarely does one hear Sidonia say she does not know anything, but she openly shared that she knew nothing about this kind of work. She got by, by watching others and doing what they did. Whenever there was confusion, she would explain that in Europe they did it a different way.

It was in Los Angeles that she met her husband, Lewis Lax. Lewis had also survived the Holocaust. Together they raised three daughters and started their own business, Classic Creations, a knitwear business in downtown Los Angeles. They celebrated much of life together, and they were involved in many Jewish organizations. They worked hard, shared core values, and appreciated every day of life.

After forty-five years of marriage, on February 8, 1994, her life partner died of a heart attack. Now she had a new challenge to shape life on her own.

Like many survivors, Sidonia took a long time to start telling her story to others.

We did not want to think about what had happened, we wanted to protect the children and we were simply too busy with life. Also, most people really had no interest in hearing the story. It is too painful.

Sidonia did everything possible to pass her values on to her children.

One, learn how to cope, no matter what life brings you. Two, always have a passport. Three, keep little things of value that can be traded for bread. Four, learn survival skills, so that you can survive under any conditions. Five, learn to be physically and psychologically strong so that you can cope with anything that comes your way.

In order to be able to stop the big fire, you have to watch for the little fire because once it burns out of control, it is too late. That means

keep up with the news. Read the news. Be active. When you see prob-
lems, get involved and stop them right at the beginning.

In 1991 Sidonia started telling her story to schoolchildren in the Los
Angeles area and has not stopped sharing her story. She talks with children
and young adults. In the past twenty-eight years she has spoken to thousands of young people in public schools, Catholic schools, and Jewish
schools, as well as university students, civic groups, and organizations.

I don't load them down with historical facts and figures. I try to com-
bine the Holocaust with moral issues and anti-racist ideas that they
can relate to.

In 2007 one of her grandsons, Joey, was a senior in a Jewish high school,
and his class was going on a trip to Poland and Israel, the March of the Living. She learned about it and was invited to participate. The core of the trip
was the experience on Holocaust Remembrance Day (Yom HaShoah),
where thousands of youth gather at Auschwitz and then walk to the neighboring camp of Birkenau. She showed the participants the bunk where she
slept with nine other women. She told them about her life there and what
happened to so many people who were not as fortunate as she. Sidonia made
this pilgrimage ten times and decided last year to take some time off. However, when one sees the treadmill at her house and hears about her exercise
regimen, it is clear she is planning to go again. In the meantime, another
grandson, David, has made a commitment to carry on her legacy and to go
each year to tell her story.

Sidonia is deeply driven by her sense of responsibility to share her personal story with others as a lens into understanding what happened to millions of people. Sidonia is all about life but is deeply mindful that the
generation of Holocaust survivors is dying out. Her mission to be with
young people is motivated by her desire to talk with them and help them
relate to a survivor.

I want to shift the paradigm of the word "Holocaust" so it represents life and not death, and how meaningful it can be when you thrive and take charge of it. Our visit to Poland is not just intended to show how people died, but how we lived. We had a rich Jewish life and community before the war. I believe you must touch people before you teach them about something. Therefore, I show them an apple before I tell my story.

Her message is about much more than just the Holocaust. It is about life. It is about an attitude of optimism. It is about taking responsibility. It is about helping others in need. It is about never giving up. At the core of her life is the love of her dad, who went to find her an apple and never came back. That apple is always with her. The Apple Lady, Sidonia, is a survivor, a refugee, an educator, a lover of life, and a woman on a mission to try to change the world so that others will never experience the horrors that she lived through.

CHAPTER 6

MALK ALAMARSH

SYRIA

The most important thing for refugees is to start their own life and pursue their own dreams. We need to help them dream again, because most of the refugees left their dreams back home. And I was one of them. I left my dream back home.

The tragedy in Syria has crushed the dreams of millions of people. In recent years, Syria has come to be known as a country of conflict, crisis, and suffering. Since the start of the Syrian civil war in 2011, countries, humanitarian groups, politicians, and media around the globe have condemned the horrific acts of violence that have plagued the country.

Although Syria had been ruled by an oppressive regime for decades, people were able to live regular lives. But many Syrians complained of high unemployment, corruption, lack of political freedom, and state repression under President Bashar al-Assad. This powder keg exploded on March 15, 2011, as a small group of protesters against the Assad regime was met with a government crackdown. Government forces responded violently to the growing pro-democracy demonstrations and used deadly force to crush the dissent. Riots broke out nationwide, demanding the president's resignation. As civilian engagement escalated, the government's repressive strong arm intensified. Malk and millions of others saw their world come to an end.

What began as a peaceful outgrowth of the Arab Spring turned into a political and religious battle involving world and regional powers. The United States and Saudi Arabia have supported the opposition, while Russia and Iran have supported the government. The complex involvement and relationship of foreign superpowers, militant rebel groups, Jihadist groups (namely ISIS [Islamic State of Iraq and Syria]), and the Syrian government have torn apart communities and families as human rights violations and violent atrocities such as airstrikes, chemical warfare, torture, and killings have claimed the lives of over 480,000 people.

Syria has been reduced to ruins, and the utter devastation from airstrikes and conflict has become the norm. The number of Syrian refugees, internally displaced persons, and lives lost is staggering, ultimately highlighting the degree to which the conflict has infiltrated the lives of innocent civilians. According to Filippo Grandi, UNHCR High Commissioner, "Syria is the biggest humanitarian and refugee crisis of our time, a continuing cause of suffering for millions which should be garnering a groundswell of support around the world."

Violence, a collapsed infrastructure, and the threat to children's lives have caused more than half of Syria's population to flee their homes. An estimated 13.6 million people have been affected by the civil war and require humanitarian assistance. More than 6 million individuals are internally displaced within Syria, and around 5.5 million have fled the country as refugees. Those that remain displaced in Syria live in informal settlements, fighting hunger and disease.

Syrians who decide to flee the country feel that they will be better off starting over in a new one. Many have seen their communities and neighborhoods attacked, their family members and friends killed. Many are victims of atrocities committed by the military-dominated government, militia forces, ISIS, and a variety of other violent partners. They have been stripped of their homeland, their cultural heritage and pride, their faith in religion, and their ability to lead a sustainable life.

The journeys to cross international borders are extremely dangerous and filled with countless risks. However, the circumstances refugees face once arriving in host and resettlement countries continue to be filled with obstacles.

Turkey, Jordan, and Lebanon have accepted most of the Syrian refugees. For the most part the refugees prefer to resettle within the European Union or the United States. But, with the exception of Germany, these countries have accepted very few refugees.

Leaving Syria and then waiting in Jordan, I didn't have the time to dream, just to survive. And if you're living without a dream, you're not alive, you are dead on the inside. You are dying inside. Being in America gave me back the ability to dream.

THE WALLS HAVE EARS

What refugees want is for people to listen to them, to see them as human beings. Many refugees cannot speak English well. It takes time. We want people to know we are really trying and willing to work very hard. The greatest gift that can be given to us is to allow us the freedom to dream again and to reclaim our lives.

A Repressive Regime Gets Harsher

War-ravaged Syria looked quite different on June 28, 1993, when Malk was born. The country was brimming with life and stability, even if under the authoritarian control of Hafez al-Assad and his Ba'ath Party. Malk's parents, Mohamed and Magida, raised their eldest child in their small home in the Jober section of Old Damascus. They lived a middle-class life. His dad was a mechanic who handled heavy-duty industrial equipment, and his mom took care of the house while working as a seamstress. Malk's sister, Rouaa, was born two years later.

It was safe, and I had the chance as all the children do, to play soccer with my friends. I could go out with them anywhere and it was safe. We didn't hear bombs or guns. We didn't hear any noises of war. We had everything—electricity, water, food. We could visit our family members without any questions, without any fear. And we could come back at night, which is something very rare in Syria right now, to come back to the house after 6:00 P.M.

I started school when I was a little kid, about five years old. I remember King Yard School. After that, I spent from grade one until grade five in middle school, and from sixth to seventh in one school and from seventh to nine in another school. The income of the teachers was very low. So they depended on private lessons to earn more money. I had a chemistry teacher who was working a second job as a taxi driver. Students had to pay for their own books and supplies and we often got a private teacher to help us prepare for the next level of education.

But in the years leading up to 2011, Malk and his family and friends were subjected to the harsh practices of Bashar al-Assad's regime, including its human rights violations, its horrible prisons and use of chemical weapons, and the lack of freedom of the press, speech, or assembly. But everyone also knew that talking about any of this was extremely dangerous.

The Ba'ath Party told the schools that they must take the students to rallies they had in their areas. They wanted to show people how the students loved Bashar al-Assad and the Ba'ath Party. I didn't have the choice, they were forcing us. It's one of the requirements in the school. We were kids and we went along with it and we enjoyed being together. We were even laughing. I didn't realize until after what it really meant. We didn't have the choice to do it or not. They would make us chant slogans about our love for Assad and how good life is in Syria.

But we would never talk about politics. It was prohibited. If anyone said anything, we would have to be careful because, as we all knew, "the walls have ears."

The Syrian TV channel was controlled by the government. They just spoke about how beautiful life was in Damascus. Watching BBC news was a crime. So was watching Al Jazeera, or Al Arabiya. But we all had the receiver to see all the channels. Al Jazeera was one of the channels that showed the truth about what was going on.

We just had to go on with our lives, and for the most part those lives were pretty good. I had many friends and activities including drawing, playing soccer, swimming, computer games and basketball. But I needed to earn money to do some of these things and to save for the future. During the summers I worked with my uncle doing electrical projects at construction sites. Then I started my own business selling balloons to children at festivals in Damascus.

But everything changed when the revolution started in 2011. I was a student, and it was very stressful, tough time for all of us. I had dropped out right before twelfth grade, the year before college, to get a private teacher to help me do well on the exams. You have to have a high grade to be able to study what you want in college. So, how well you did on the exams decided your future career. I didn't think that I was going to do well on the test even though I studied for three months for the exams, eighteen hours a day. I received an 86.4 out of 100. I wanted to study mechanical engineering or architecture but I was told I could be a dental assistant, and I began to study that at Damascus University.

I started to realize that life is not easy because of the government. I learned that you don't have the choice to study what you want, that for any paperwork connected to anything with the government, you must bribe. Even if you are driving and the police officer stopped you, you must bribe him. Al Jazeera showed the problems. The Al Jazeera channel, it was the main part of the Syrian Revolution.

The Revolution Begins

In March 2011, a "Day of Rage" demonstration was held in the southern city of Daraa, where fifty protesters were killed for demanding the release of political prisoners. Those jailed and tortured were mainly high school students who had painted anti-government graffiti on walls throughout the area. In response, a "Day of Dignity" general strike and rallies, which Malk attended, were held throughout the country in December.

It was scary and frightening, but also exciting. It was a great moment for me because I could finally say anything from my heart against the dictator without being judged or without being scared. I felt I finally had a voice and could express it. The rally was intended to be peaceful, asking for freedom, asking for those students who were in jail to be freed. It was a time I will never forget because I was proud of what we were doing and had hope that it would lead to change.

However, those hopes were quickly dashed by a brutal regime. Malk saw horrendous violence against the student leaders of the demonstrations.

The secret police seemed to be everywhere. They took many children and teens away to jail and tortured them. Then the parents were blamed that they had not raised their children right. They went to the local sheikh, who functioned as a mayor, begging for help in getting their children released.

Malk's father was arrested. There were no charges; it was just a random arrest of people in the area. He was jailed for twelve days and severely beaten. He came out with broken bones and no teeth. Although his father did not talk about what happened, Malk saw videos of what they did to prisoners and how they forced them onto the ground in front of Assad's picture and made them pray to him.

In early 2012 I was arrested. A friend and I were having an argument with another student. I was talking about Facebook, how the government was using Facebook and had accessibility to Facebook to control people and ask them and question them if they go above or if they go beyond the red line. The guy I was talking to was actually Secret Police. There were many students on campus who were. More police came over and asked me for my ID, which showed that I lived in Jober, an area of Damascus where the revolution had started, so they asked me to open my Facebook page. I refused. I said I didn't have one. But one of my friends, they saw some videos on his phone, rally videos, the revolution. He was going to upload it to YouTube, to show the world what's going on. They caught him, they forced him to open his Facebook page, and they found me on his friends list. When they opened my page I had a post that said shame on you Hafez al-Assad, the father. They took us inside a building and they started beating us, questioning us.

Finally, they offered us a deal. They wanted me to be a secret reporter in the college. I said yes of course. They told me they would give me whatever I wanted, fake IDs, different names, and money and girls. Anything I wanted. I said, yes of course, tomorrow morning I will be here. Since then I stopped going to the college. I didn't come back. I never showed up again.

I would rather die than go to a prison in Syria.

Malk could not go home as he knew he would be arrested. So, he went into hiding for two months, going from friend to friend, city to city. His life was at risk. There was intense fighting in Jober and neighboring areas. During Ramadan in 2012, helicopters started to drop bombs throughout residential areas of Damascus, killing many people.

My world had completely changed. Everything had changed. All my choices had changed, everything became about surviving, me and my family, and supporting them, because my dad couldn't. At this point he couldn't go to his work. What Bashar did, what the government did, they put checkpoints separating each part of the city from the others. And each checkpoint had guns, men and tanks and bombs, everything.

Staying Alive by Getting to Jordan

Malk had to flee the country but needed a passport. Getting one is a long, bureaucratic process, but with the help of some friends and several bribes he secured one after a few weeks. He found people who were willing to take him out of the country to Jordan. It meant more bribes, more risk, more danger. But the Jordanian authorities turned him away because he did not have any relatives there.

Malk returned to Syria and remained in hiding for a few months. Desperate to cross the border, he found a taxi driver known for being able to do just that. After a dangerous journey and many more bribes, the driver told the Jordanian authorities that Malk was going to study in Amman. It worked. Malk arrived in Amman with twenty Jordanian *dinars*, about thirty-five dollars, to his name. Within a day, he got a job in a coffee shop. He was paid terrible wages and survived only by staying with friends. He had left behind his country, his family, his studies, everything he knew, and worked twelve hours a day to earn money for food.

I was nineteen years old and I hated the life I was living. I was forced to live like this to survive. There were no dreams, there was no future, it's just surviving each day. We eat today, that's fine. I even had times in Jordan, when we didn't have anything in the refrigerator. When I was working in a men's clothing shop, and they were ordering from fast food restaurants, I didn't have money to order there. I would eat their leftovers.

Malk saved every cent he could to help get his parents and sister to Jordan. That was all he wanted. He would often go hungry for days, sleeping on the floors of friends' apartments. Finally, his mom and sister got passports and were able to join him. It took another year for his dad to rejoin the family.

I heard news about Syria from my family back home and they were just surviving. At some point I lost my cousin. The government burned her house. She was ten years old, she was a child. I have a friend who died in jail. He was arrested for three and a half years, for no reason. All this made me realize that no matter how hard the work in Jordan, how tough the life, I just had to be responsible, and smart enough to get money to provide my family in the hope to get out of Jordan. I wasn't going to stay here. I needed to get out. Because I started realizing how some of the people here are racist against Syrian people. Jordan is a great place to visit, but it's a war country and not safe for the refugee.

In 2013, the family registered with the UNHCR for refugee status. The process would take three long years. During that time, there were many interviews and extensive background checks. Obtaining refugee status is a tremendous challenge. Being a Muslim from Syria made the visa application process for the United States much more demanding. The vetting is extremely thorough.

The woman at the police department in Jordan whom Malk was working with for his refugee ID was not helpful and at one point did not show up for work for two months. When she finally returned, Malk asked what was going on. She told him that he was a Syrian refugee and not entitled to ask questions.

I was totally powerless. I forced myself to be nice to her even though all I really wanted to do was to yell at her. The way she spoke to us was like we were low, and she's controlling us somehow.

Malk and his family rented a simple place, and Malk worked fifteen-hour days in a restaurant to support them. His sister landed a job, and his mother started working again as a seamstress. Malk's father was initially unable to work because of the mental and physical trauma he suffered from his imprisonment, but he eventually got a job as a mechanic.

What happens next? I started looking for something I'm interested in, to work. Because each one in the family has his own job, providing enough money for the home and everything. So I started looking for a career, actually. A career for my life. And I found that my friend, a friend from college who had been a roommate was working at a cell phone shop, and he could get me in. And I became a cell phone technician. At first, I was learning, working like an intern. But after one year I started working by myself as a technician. I started fixing phones, I started showing my skills in customer service. I had learned so much and had more knowledge and more information than when I started working. I specialized in Apple phones. I did this for more than two years.

I was telling myself, "I'm going to start my life. I'm going to start dreaming, start learning and working." And I read about life in the United States, how beautiful. If you are hardworking, you will get results of your hard work, and not stay where you are. That's the point I was missing in Jordan. Keep working hard, and stay where you are.

*No improvement, no promotion, either from the job or the life. I was
thinking about the moment when I would leave Jordan and travel to
the United States.*

In July 2016, as he did every day, he checked his application online, and
there appeared the word that had only been a dream: Approved. They got
notice that they would leave in a week. The family sold their furniture and
lived in an empty home to get ready for their trip to America. But hours
before their scheduled departure, Malk received a call that their flight had
been canceled. They got no further information.

Powerless, he and his family lived in the empty house with no jobs.
Neighbors provided them with food.

*I used the time to see and say goodbye to all my friends in Jordan. So
many people had helped me, and I wanted to spend time with them
before leaving.*

He remained optimistic although he knew that the flight might never
be rescheduled and that they might need to remain in Jordan.

In two weeks they got rebooked and learned that their destination was
Atlanta, where they knew no one. Malk researched it and saw the Coca-
Cola headquarters and the Atlanta aquarium. That was enough to again
buoy his spirits about the journey ahead. On August 15, 2016, Malk and
his family arrived in Atlanta to start their new life.

Finding Safety in America

*I was filled with sadness about leaving the life I had loved growing up
in Damascus. That is where I thought I would always live. However,
that all came to an end, I want to forget about the horrors of Syria and
the tough years in Jordan. Now, I was in America, with so many freedom and choices. I knew, that if I worked hard enough, I had the
opportunity to shape a good life here.*

After a 3:00 A.M. stop at a Waffle House, they were taken to a small
apartment in Clarkston.

It was great. Tiny and with two levels. It was a great moment. I didn't care where I would live, how it was decorated or how big it was. I didn't care about any of it. I was happy and grateful and thankful for being here in the United States. And I realized that my life had just started. I don't know, like, I was reborn again. The beginning of my new life.

I started improving my English, started introducing myself to the neighbors, to the community. Started looking for a job and asking for help to get a job. World Relief was really helping us with paperwork. I started studying. I started going to school. And then I got a job at Refuge Coffee in Clarkston.

About thirty minutes from downtown Atlanta, Clarkston is a small city that had fallen on tough times. It was originally built to house Atlanta airport employees. However, they moved to the suburbs. City leaders decided to welcome refugees into their community as they had a lot of available housing. It has become known as "the most diverse square mile in America" and the "Ellis Island of the South." Around Clarkston, it is easy to spot nearly a dozen refugee communities in apartment complexes, and the strip malls all have businesses that cater to the influx.

To support our family, my mom and I started a catering company, Suryana Cuisine. We started it two years ago. I am the CEO and director of operations and the business continues to expand. We were thinking about doing the same thing that Refuge Coffee does, helping refugees, providing them living wages, and working with them. So we built our business on this idea. One day I hope to go to Georgia State and study computer science or business.

When they get catering jobs, they employ other Syrian refugees who help prepare Syrian and Middle Eastern dishes. One man who recently used the catering company said Malk and Magida provided excellent food, wonderful service, "and the meal is enhanced with their authenticity and care. Everyone enjoys meeting them."

Malk's networking skills help the catering business. He seems to know everyone. In mid-2017, with everyone working, the family moved to a home in Stone Mountain, Georgia. There, the streets reflect the diversity of America: African Americans, white Americans, Somalis, Iraqis, and Afghanis. Like most refugees, Malk's parents have a social network that is all Syrian, speaking Arabic and sticking to themselves. It would be a hard transition for anyone their age. They are grateful to America, but their source of comfort comes from their community. Malk is engaged in American society, with many friends, and is acculturating to the system that will allow him to succeed here.

Malk has already accomplished so much. Many Americans are sympathetic to refugees, he said, but a lot of people do not understand refugees, especially those from Syria.

Refugees have been through tough times. They are hard workers, and smart, and they just need a safe place where they can become productive, for the community, for their family and for the country. The biggest challenge, here in the United States when they first come, is the language. When you work with someone who speaks your language, it's not hard because they understand each other. We do like to keep the culture, and to keep our traditions, to keep the language as well, our language. I'm still struggling with the English language as well. It's difficult. But for many, it's more difficult because some of them can't go to school because of their full-time job. Some of them don't have enough time to go to school to learn English. And some of them, they don't realize how important it is to know English. You have to speak it.

For the refugee, everything has changed. So being patient and help them, these are the two most important things. And listen to them. The most important thing for the refugee is to start his own life, his own dream. Help them to dream again, because the majority of the refugees, they left their dreams back home.

Like refugees throughout America, he and his family are trying to shape a new life based on the best of American values: freedom, equality, and the ability to shape one's own life through hard work. Malk is mature beyond his years. At twenty-five, he takes every opportunity he can to learn about other people, American culture, and business. Before coming to America, he had never met a Jew. He now understands much more about Judaism and other religions. Malk wants to fully integrate into American life while holding onto his family, cultural, and religious traditions.

Most of my family is still in Syria. They are trying their best to live each day and survive the nightmare of Syria. No one posts anything on Facebook about the situation, and even I don't from America. No one knows what this regime will do.

A passionate and intelligent man, Malk has little awareness of the controversial history surrounding the imposing mountain of rock near their home. It is Stone Mountain, where the second Ku Klux Klan was born in 1915. Carved into the mountainside are images of heroes of the Confederacy: Jefferson Davis, Robert E. Lee, and Stonewall Jackson.

What matters most to me is that the nightmare of Syria is over for me and my family, and I am beginning to pursue the American dream. It will take time and hard work.

Malk is on the path to citizenship. He wants to be a well-informed, independent, responsible, and contributing member of society. There does not seem to be much that will hold this young man back from achieving his dreams.

CHAPTER 7

VANNY LOUN

CAMBODIA

I remember an old man saying to my mum: "You know when your
house gets robbed, you still have a house, you still have furniture. But
when your house gets bombed and burnt, you don't have anything.
You are homeless, you are just lucky to be alive." Since that day, I never
saw my village, but I always wanted to go home. My mum never took
me back.

Like so many other Cambodians, Vanny Loun saw her house and life
destroyed by the genocidal actions of the Khmer Rouge (the army of the
Cambodian Communist Party) in the last half of the 1970s. But the area
that is now called Cambodia has a centuries-old history as an important
trade route linking China to India and Southeast Asia. The kingdoms
of Cambodia were influenced by many cultures and enjoyed centuries of
prosperity followed by hundreds of years of suffering and demise. In more
recent years, Cambodia gained its independence from France in 1953 but
was never really able to emerge into a free and vibrant society. During the
Vietnam War, Cambodia tried to remain neutral, but the United States
felt that the Vietcong were using the Cambodian countryside as staging
areas for attacks. In the early 1970s the United States embarked on a long
period of heavy bombing in Cambodia, killing well over a hundred thousand people.

The end of the Vietnam War and the heavy toll that Cambodia experienced during this era gave rise to the brutal guerrilla movement of Pol Pot
and the Khmer Rouge regime. His goal was to create an agrarian socialist
society. The regime seized complete power of the country in 1975 and instituted a series of measures that were intended to indoctrinate a new generation of Cambodians. The people were promised a utopian society where
everyone would be equal and prosper. However, that dream was quickly
shattered when the Khmer Rouge isolated itself from the world, expelled
all foreign media, and embarked on a four-year-long genocide from 1975
to 1979. Money, schools, companies, hospitals, and the basic underpinnings

of modern society were made obsolete. Doctors, lawyers, bankers, educators, and intellectuals were the first to be exterminated and forced into exile. Millions of Cambodians were forced out of cities to work on collective farms under brutal conditions. Many of these people died from starvation, executions, forced labor, and basic diseases that could no longer be treated since all of the doctors had been exterminated. To put the sheer horror and magnitude of this atrocity into perspective, an estimated 21 percent of the country's population, about 1.7–2 million Cambodians, was killed during the Khmer Rouge's four years in power. The groups most targeted in the genocide were Buddhists, Muslims, Christians, ethnic Chinese, Vietnamese, Thai, and Cambodians with Chinese, Vietnamese, or Thai ancestry.

Finally, in 1979, Vietnam liberated Cambodia from the brutal regime of the Khmer Rouge. The genocide ended, but for many of the survivors, like Vanny, the horrors did not. The peaceful world of their childhood had been destroyed, leaving them scarred and traumatized for years to come.

My memories of Cambodia are with me day and night. I see all the people getting killed, my friends being tortured, and horrific images of people being shot. I keep thinking about why these images will not leave me alone. The ones I want to know, to remember, they don't come to my head. It is just the horrors of the past that come to me. And I'm so upset. I just want to go jump in the ocean and die. I am grateful that my family and a few other people have given me the desire to stay alive, trying my best to rid myself of the demons.

A River of Memories

The first ten years of my life were happy and good. Everything changed when we were bombed in 1969. I was growing up in a small village near Battambang and had everything I needed: my mom, my dad, my grandparents and lots of land. The house was far away from any neighbors. We were surrounded by lots of trees: coconut, mango, banana and orange trees. I recall as a child spending hours climbing trees.

The Accidental Bombing

Vanny was born on June 1, 1959. As she tells her story, only the second time she has ever done so, one can feel the depths of her joy and her pain. Her children will learn her story when they read it.

As a child I was outgoing and always smiled. I loved to sing. I would sing a lot. I also enjoyed dancing. "Look at that girl," people would say, "she's so small and she's singing, singing." I remember that. I loved to sing and dance, and every day was so happy.

Her smile remains radiant. She tells her story in English that is good but not fluent. She is diminutive in physical stature but large in character and courage. She talks openly about the mental anguish, the post-traumatic stress disorder (PTSD) she has been living with for the past seven years as the nightmares of her childhood emerge. Yet somehow, she can share her story.

Her parents, Lon Sing and Lumang Sok, raised her in the village of Mau Din, where she was safe and all her needs were provided for. The houses did not have electricity, but they did have clean water. Her father was in the army and often gone for long periods of time. His salary supported the family as her mother took care of Vanny and her sister and later two more daughters.

They had a beautiful garden and lots of land. As a child, she played with the other children and took daily walks with her grandfather into the mountains to pick vegetables. Vanny's fondest memories are the many trips she took with her mom to Phnom Penh, Angkor Wat, and Battambang, as well as other cities. They enjoyed their time seeing relatives, exploring, going into stores, and taking in a movie.

In Phnom Penh, I had many cousins to play with. We would play in the river all day. We would go for one week, then come home, and two or three weeks later we'd go again. Then we went to Angkor Wat where we met aunties and uncles and more cousins. I remember we sat on top of an elephant. The elephant had a big basket on top of its back, and it fit three people in the basket, and we all rode the elephant around Angkor Wat. We had so much fun.

I spent a few years in school and all I remember is how strict the teachers were. Oh, you cannot write, they would say. You write it wrong. I whip you, your hand. Put the hand right there. Then the teacher whips you with a bamboo stick. I was in such pain. I never wanted to go back to school. I am so grateful that my mom did not make me go and we would make our trips instead.

Although my grandfather begged us not to take another trip, we wanted to go to Phnom Penh to see family. I will never forget how he said to us, "Stay here in your house, and your land and your village. I'm too old now. I'm so tired, just please don't go out too much." My mum said, "Okay, we will go this time, and when I come back, we will stay home more."

Three days later in Phnom Penh, I heard my mom and my auntie screaming. They had been listening to the radio and learned that our village had been bombed. They bombed the Vietcong, but they also bombed our village by mistake. And my mum cried, and then she said, "Stay here with auntie and your cousins and I am going to go home and see what happened." She returned after five days. She looked so sad and different. I just said, "Mum, what's going on mum?" And she just looked at me. She said, "Kid, your grandparents

are dead. The bomb dropped in front of our door. The house has been
destroyed."

My mum said, "It's not only us, everybody in that village, many of
our friends had been killed or injured. Those who could, ran away
from the village to the jungle." I missed my grandparents so much, I
didn't know what to do, didn't know what to say, but cry. I still wanted
to go home, but mum said we had no home to go to. I still could see
my house, my grandparents in my mind. But my mum kept explain-
ing they were gone. Burned to the ground and gone.

Struggling to Survive during the Rise of Pol Pot

They stayed in Phnom Penh for a while after the bombing. They then
moved to Bipad, near the Thailand border, where her dad was stationed.
She and her mother would prepare food at home and sell it in the local
market. Their world became one of poverty and subsistence. With barely
enough food, they moved from house to house, struggling to find enough
money to survive.

> *My mum became so sad. And every day when I went to school I*
> *couldn't hear what the teacher said. After school I came home, and*
> *I climbed a mango tree near the house, like I did in my village. I*
> *would sit there for hours until my mum called me to come down. All*
> *I remember is how poor we were and how sad I was all the time.*
>
> *And my mom had to sell everything at the local market. I would*
> *go with her, and Daddy would go to work. And then every day we*
> *would earn a little bit more. Later I got a pillow and then a blanket.*
> *It was so cold at night. But we had the roof over our heads.*

Vanny's dad was promoted many times in the army, and in early 1973,
when Vanny was thirteen, her family moved to Battambang. But Vanny
was taken to live with her cousins in Phnom Penh for a year. There she
flourished. She began to heal from the bombing and felt hopeful about the
future of Cambodia. After she returned to Battambang, her cousins would

come to see her. They would share with her the stories of the fighting, the bombings, and their life in the military. She could observe them in military training. In the early 1970s, the United States greatly increased its bombing in Cambodia with the justification that it believed the Vietcong were hiding there.

Meanwhile, Pol Pot, the revolutionary leader, was gaining strength in his attempt to overthrow the government of Cambodia and start his own communist state. He and his men were out in the jungles fighting the Cambodian army and increasing their vitriolic rhetoric against the Western influence in Cambodia and how it was eroding Cambodian society. Pol Pot's promise was to build a new and equal society in Cambodia, and he was gaining more supporters, especially as the American bombings increased.

Vanny, and most of the Cambodian people, did not have access to news about Cambodia. All television and media were controlled by the state.

In 1975, there was great joy in Cambodia with the Vietnam War coming to an end. Initially, the people of Cambodia thought that Pol Pot and the Khmer Rouge would help rebuild the Cambodia of Vanny's childhood.

I was fifteen, about to be sixteen, when the Khmer Rouge came in. We were so happy. We felt there would be no more war. I ran to the army place to find my father and my cousins. I saw that all the Khmer Rouge had guns, but the Cambodian soldiers had no guns. They had taken their guns away. And they made them sit on the big black trucks. We were worried they were going to take them away.

The KR were walking around with their guns yelling orders at the men in the trucks. The men in the trucks looked miserable. The KR yelled at me and the other women: "Hey, we need some food. Go tell all the people in this village to cook and bring the food to us." I ran home, with my mom and sisters, and prepared food to bring back to them.

And then, the next day we made food again and brought it to them, but the trucks were gone. The KR soldiers took the food, and told us to go home and pack, that we would be gone three days, but we had to leave because America was going to come and bomb all of us. So we packed right away. When we came back, the scene was total chaos. The KR separated my mom and two sisters from my little sister and me. I could not get to my mom; my mom could not get to me. They just pointed the gun at us and said go this way, and told my mom to go that way. I tried to tell them that my sister was only four years old.

Betrayal and Brutality of the Khmer Rouge

We walked for three days with hundreds of other people. We arrived at a village called High Jungle. It was a village filled with people that I had never seen before. They were dark skinned and had their own huts. They spoke a different kind of Cambodian that I did not understand. They did not do anything to help us. They were called Khmer Phnom, mountain people.

The KR just left us there. The village people kept watching us like we were prisoners. We made shacks from wood to sleep in. We shared sheets. We had to find food in a field, anything we could pick, anything that grew. We boiled it and ate it. There was no rice. Most of us had little food and were getting sick. I saw many people die. And my neck, it was getting long, so skinny like bones and skin. And my sister, she looked like a skeleton. And every day we hugged each other and wondered, Are we going to die today?

We saw people eat their own kids who had died.

For almost six months, we lived outside the village. Every day more people came. And more people died. I was doing everything I could to keep my sister and me alive.

One day I saw Khmer Rouge soldiers and decided to go to them. "Mitt bong," I said, to one soldier who was playing with his gun. Mitt bong means friend, which they liked us to call them. "Mitt bong, can

I have some rice?" I asked him. He stopped playing with his gun, and he looked at me for a long time. Then he said, "Give her some rice." Then, they gave me rice, a little rice, that we made last for the whole month.

Six months passed. Then a new Khmer Rouge leader came and told us that we would work every day and they would feed us. They told us to go, make rice fields, plant vegetables, everything. And then they made us rice soup, a little bit rice and a lot of water, and that's all we had. And we just drank that soup and went back to work. We worked twelve hours every day.

They told us to make our clothes look black. We picked some fruit that makes black, and we pounded that fruit, and it turned black color. And then we put all the clothes in there, and over night our clothes turned ugly.

They had first said we would be gone three days and then go home. Now we had been here for six months and we had a job now, we had a group we were close to, we went to work, everything. So, one day a Khmer Rouge came and sat by my side and asked me for some water. I gave him the water, and I said, "Mitt bong, when are they going let us go back home?" He looked at me and said, "You will never go back home." He was nice to tell me the truth. "You will never go back home."

And so Vanny understood that this was life now. She would wake every morning to go to work in the rice paddies that were muddy after the rains.

I was the youngest in the group. My sister would stay behind in the hut while I worked. The ground was so muddy that I would fall, get up and go again. Then I would fall again. A friend who worked with me would keep saying to get up, let's go, because the soldiers are not happy when you keep falling down. It slows us down. There was no talking, no falling, you had to walk fast, work very fast. And every day, even Saturday and Sunday. Twelve hours a day. And still there was not enough food to eat.

I fell so much that they beat me. But I had to keep working. Plant some rice like this: put my thumb in rice, put it in the mud, and cover it, take another one, put it in, and cover it. But the leeches kept coming to my legs. But a guy would come and just grab the leech, and throw it away, and he would go to work again. He didn't say anything, but every day he would come and help me with the leeches. The Khmer Rouge would watch from the treetops where they sat with their guns. We were prisoners.

One day, I was walking home and I saw a banana, hanging low on a tree. I looked and there was nobody to see, so I grabbed three bananas and went straight home. And then in the morning, the lady in charge of the cafeteria called for me. She knew I picked the bananas, and she yelled at me saying I was a rich spoiled kid, and she beat me with the wood used for firewood. She kept beating me on my head again and again. All I could see were stars. She beat me and beat me. It was big and swollen.

She made me stay until the next day when the big boss was back from another village. The lady told him that I can't do anything right. I was only sixteen then. The guy asked me if my dad was a soldier. I told him the truth. Yes, I said, he had been on one of those trucks. He was quiet. He knew my dad had been killed. So he told me to go home and get back to work. He saved my life. He could have killed me. The lady was sent to another village. But my head got worse and worse. I had a seizure. A guy made me medicine from a tree leaf and it brought my fever down.

I had worked in the fields for a year. But then the big boss sent me to work with the elderly in the factory to make clothing. I worked there for another year.

People died every day. They would get sick, and with no medicine they would die. People who had come with me, who I knew from my old village, who had walked together with me, disappeared. The soldiers took them to the jungle and they never returned. We all saw them. But the commander would not tell us, the soldiers didn't talk to us at all. So where did these people go? They were just gone. We cannot ask anyone a question. We just saw and remained quiet. We knew that tomorrow it might be us who are taken out to the jungle.

Vanny's Voice Saves Lives

There was new KR leadership and Vanny was sent to work in the vegetable gardens. One day she came home to find her sister gone. Her neighbor told her that her sister had been taken away. So Vanny walked five miles to where her sister was being held.

"Mitt bong, mitt bong, please let my sister come home with me. I have only my sister. I don't have anyone else," I said. And the woman did not say nothing. She looked so mean. She looked at me for a while with that vicious and mean face. And then she said, "Yeah, take her." My friends could not believe that I had the courage to do this. For me, there was no choice. I had to get my sister or she was going to die.

In her hut Vanny kept a bowl containing the herbal medicine that had been prepared for her after the severe beating. One night when she returned home, it was gone.

Every day the KR searched all the huts looking for anything they could find and decided to take that bowl. That bowl was my life. Somehow, I managed to go to the warehouse to talk to the woman who took it. She tells me that no one can have medicine. One of the big boss soldiers was listening. The next day, the woman was sent to another village where she became a worker like me.

Vanny could have been killed any of the times she spoke up. Yet she never stopped using her voice to fight for her life. Listening to her tell me her stories, it hits me how I wish Vanny could talk to people everywhere about finding the courage to use the power of one's voice.

The years went by and Vanny turned eighteen. She had one very close friend, Keni.

One day, while in the rice fields I saw my best friend with two soldiers, her hands tied behind her, and all she could say was, "Goodbye, Vanny, goodbye." And she was walked into the jungle. Later, those two guys came back and they laughed as they told the story of raping and killing Keni.

Every day I kept looking at the sky and asked the Americans to come back, please come back. Please come back and help us. We are all going to die here. America, please come back.

A few days after Keni was killed, a new battalion of KR soldiers took over. They called a meeting and told the people that there had been enough killing and that things needed to change. They would no longer carry guns. The new leader asked for Vanny. He told her how fortunate she was. He had found a book kept by the former KR leaders with a list of those to be killed within a few days, and she was on it.

For the next six months the working conditions were much more humane, the food was better, and she was no longer living under constant threat. In 1979, they heard gunshots every day and learned that it was the Vietnamese army getting closer to liberate Cambodia from the KR.

I had been here for four years. No shampoo. No soap. No toothbrush. With only the clothes that we brought from home.

We were all very happy because we had thought we were going to die, but then the Vietnamese came. They told us that we could go any-where we wanted. We could leave. We heard that we might get help at the Thai border. We walked for weeks through the jungle. We slept on the ground under a tree. Then I met a man who said he knew my mom. When he left he told my mom that I was on the road. She came with my two other sisters and we were together for the first time in four years.

*From there it was only one day and one night to the Thailand bor-
der. We walked all night and arrived at a fence at sunrise. A soldier
was there, and he pointed his gun at us and told us not to pass the
fence, or he would kill us. The Americans were nowhere to be seen. But
a day later, one American appeared on the Thai side and promised to
bring help. After a week, the United Nations arrived with food, tents,
pots and other supplies. We were told to stay there while a refugee
camp was being built in Thailand. For a year, we were left by the fence,
surviving with help from the U.N.*

*Then we moved to the camp and got a house. When we moved in,
we filled out papers that would help us get to America. Every week
the names of people going were put up on a board. We were there
for two years before we read our names on the list. But until then, we
went to school to learn English, had doctors, had enough food, and
were taken care of.*

*My mom went first, to Oakland, California. I originally had four
sisters. One died on a boat trying to escape Cambodia, and one was
taken by the Khmer Rouge and we never saw her again. My two
surviving sisters and I went later to Des Moines, Iowa. When we got
off the plane, our sponsors, Catholic people, took us to our apartment. It had rooms, beds, food, and clothes and everything we
needed.*

We were there for four years.

*I went to adult school to learn English, the government paid our
rent, and the Catholic relief brought us food and clothes. We watched
TV, cooked Cambodian food, and talked to a few other Cambodian
people.*

*I was happy to be in America. But I was sad about all that hap-
pened. I wanted to be with my mom. So when my English was better,
I told someone I wanted to go to Oakland. He introduced me to a social
worker who made the arrangements. So in 1985, we were all united
again with our mother.*

I continued to study English and got a job working at Motel 6 doing housekeeping. Then I became a day care provider. In 1988 I married an American man and together we had four children. Twenty years later we were divorced. During those twenty years I raised the children, managed the house and continued to run a day care center. During those years I did not think about Cambodia and remembered very little.

The River of Memories Runs Deep with Pain

In 2010 I started having nightmares, all the memories flooding back. I could not bear it. All I did was cry. I was just so sad and sometimes I just wanted to die.

Vanny learned about a wonderful organization, Center for Empowering Refugees and Immigrants (CERI), in Oakland and started going there to meet with a social worker and to spend time with other Cambodian women.

After a while I started to talk to my caseworker and that has been so important in my life. The nightmares continue and often I just sit in a room and cry. I remember the river in my home village which I loved because I had so much fun there with my cousins, all who were killed by the KR. Those who died don't know what happened to me. Now I go to the San Francisco Bay and I stand and look out at the ocean, and I scream, "Cousins!" I want them to know that I am alive and that I raised a family. I'm in America. Cousin. Grandma. Grandpa. Daddy, I'm in America. I'm safe.

Vanny now lives with her children, who are grown and holding good jobs, in Oakland. She is unable to work because of her PTSD. She says that the only way to soothe the pain is to stay in her room and listen to loud music. A few times a month her children take her to Lake Tahoe, where she likes to just sit and listen to the water. This is her only real relief from the haunting images of her life in Cambodia.

Around the time the nightmares began, she and her sister returned to Cambodia. The village of their childhood is gone and is now part of the jungle. She returned to Phnom Penh, which she describes as broken. They spent two weeks there. She felt good about being back in her home but terrible about the life that was destroyed.

Vanny has eight grandchildren ranging in age from two to twenty. It is clear how much she loves her family, but when her demons haunt her, it is hard for her to enjoy them. Her children married Americans. They have never been to Cambodia. They only recently learned the story of what she experienced in Cambodia.

Her life revolves around her weekly visit to CERI, where she talks with other women, takes Zumba dancing lessons, and meets with her social workers. Vanny loves watching movies at home, especially old cowboy movies and James Bond films.

She dreams the demons will go away so that she can enjoy her life and her family. She is deeply grateful to America for giving her refuge, and she wants that same refuge from her nightmares. She has already added so much to our country with her children and grandchildren, in whom she has infused the values of kindness, hard work, courage, respect, and love.

Right now, I'm okay. And my children, my life and my soul, I love them very much. I would die for them if I had to. America saved me. They saved my two sisters too, and all the people. And we live in America, we all have a good life. We have support everywhere. We have everything to learn if you want to learn. I wish the nightmares would go away. However, they stay with me all the time.

CHAPTER 8

DARWIN VELASQUEZ

EL SALVADOR

*I was born in La Union, El Salvador where I spent the first twelve years
of my life. In 2005, my parents left El Salvador to escape violence and
to give us a better life. Our grandparents took care of us. Two years
later, I received a call from my father who was in the U.S. telling me I
was leaving El Salvador the very next day. There was no explanation.
It wasn't a choice.*

Darwin Velasquez was most fortunate to enter the country when he did
in 2007. The 2018 "Zero Tolerance" Trump policy and all the surrounding
issues of life in detention centers, treatment of minors, separation of families, and lack of attorneys to help people seeking asylum have made life
increasingly more difficult for El Salvadorans on the migrant trail. For
many people, staying in El Salvador is no longer an option, given the esca-
lation of intolerable violence and poverty.

Plagued by the country's history of drug cartels, gangs, and a long civil
war, El Salvador's citizens have experienced homicidal violence that has
resulted in a wave of refugee movement to the United States. El Salvador,
along with its neighbors Honduras and Guatemala, makes up part of Central America's "Northern Triangle." Throughout the years, this region
has been recognized as the murder capital of the world; El Salvador reached
an all-time high in 2015 with 104 murders per 100,000 people. Since then
it has improved with a decreased murder rate of 50.3 per 100,000. The
country's history of political upheaval, corrupt government antics, sav-
age gang activity, and organized crime has left many El Salvadorans,
most notably women and children, like Darwin and his family, no viable
option for survival other than fleeing the country.

El Salvador was engulfed in a civil war between 1980 and 1991 that
plunged El Salvadoran society into violence and left several thousands of
people dead. Postwar criminal activity gave rise to street gangs, commonly
known as *maras*. Most notable are the Mara Salvatrucha 13 and 18th Street,
whose growth has been attributed to many factors, including poverty,

government instability, access to weapons from the civil war, and lack of access to basic services and educational opportunities. These dominant gangs participate in kidnappings, extortion, drug trafficking, and planned assassinations, while targeting the country's youth population for gang 'recruitment. The origins of both gangs reside in El Salvadorans who had fled to Los Angeles for a better life, learned the techniques of Latino and other gangs, and then were deported.

When asked why they left their home, 59 percent of Salvadoran boys and 61 percent of Salvadoran girls list crime, gang threats, or violence as a reason for their emigration. Whereas males most feared assault or death for not joining gangs or interacting with corrupt government officials, females most feared rape or disappearance at the hands of the same groups.

Such horrific realities have left parents and guardians in distress. They are forced to weigh the risks of a dangerous journey to the United States with an uncertain future versus the prevailing dangers of staying in El Salvador.

The phenomenon of the unaccompanied alien child (UAC)—defined in statute as an alien under age eighteen who lacks lawful immigration status in the United States, and who is without a parent or legal guardian in the United States or lacks a parent or legal guardian in the United States who is available to provide care and physical custody—is staggering, with 50,036 UAC apprehensions by the U.S. Border Patrol in just 2018 alone. Upon arrival to the United States, and given the circumstances these children are fleeing (violence, deprivation, abuse, etc.), humanitarian forms of immigration relief are desperately needed.

Darwin is a beneficiary of the DACA (Deferred Action for Childhood Arrivals) program, established in 2012 by the Obama administration. At this point, the future of DACA beneficiaries is uncertain. Darwin is just one of the hundreds of thousands who are already contributing to life in America.

Blind but the Heart Can See

If I had never come to America, I would have married and had kids
at a very young age, and my education would have stopped at the fifth
grade. My visual impairment would be worse. I would be connected
to a gang, or living in fear of them or the government. Every day would
pose the threat of death. Here, the only thing I worry about is that a
change in policy would lead to deportation.

Difficult Family Decisions

Darwin was born blind in the small village of La Union, El Salvador. With
only 2,000 people, and four hours away by dirt road from the capital of
San Salvador, there was no access to medical care in the area. So it was
not until the age of six that he had the first of ten surgeries in each eye.

Darwin's parents and brother taught him the alphabet by using chalk
to draw in very big letters on the door. From an early age, he compensated
for his loss of sight by memorizing everything. His first surgery was life
changing.

Then I could see a little bit. I could see my parents, I could see their
faces, I could see. I could see my friends. It was like re-learning the
world around me from a physical perspective because before, I would
recognize my Dad, but it was more on the hearing of his voice. And
even today, people who yell "Hi!" to me from behind, I know who it is
because of my hearing, which is still very good. I am able to somehow
distinguish people's voices.

My earliest memory is playing soccer, street soccer. We would put
two rocks and that would be the goal with another two rocks on the
opposite side. I remember growing up with a lot of friends, a lot of close
friends. Many of them have unfortunately died, killed by violence as
gang members or killed because they wouldn't join.

Darwin's dad, Pedro (a pseudonym to protect him from Immigration and Customs Enforcement [ICE]), was a contractor building ports and freeways throughout the country. He would be gone for long periods of time. La Union is a very poor village, and as his dad only returned on occasion, his mom needed to bring in money for them to survive.

Mom, my brother and I used to have our little business because Mom never liked to depend on Dad, as he was gone most of the time. We sold fish, avocados, and cow meat to neighboring towns for us to have sufficient money to survive. Our biggest fear was that the gangs would take the money away from us.

Darwin started school in kindergarten, as his parents felt education was of the utmost importance.

Dad didn't know how to read. He learned when he started going to church. Mom only got to finish seventh grade. So, they always viewed education as a key to doors of opportunities.

The school did not make any accommodations for students with disabilities. People with disabilities simply did not go to school, as there was no support of any kind. However, Darwin's brother Mario helped him with everything, as even after the surgeries, his sight remained limited in terms of reading. All the supplies for school—uniforms, books, pens and paper—had to be purchased. Darwin's family was able to afford that.

My brother had to help me with my homework. I'm so thankful to him. He is part of the reason that I graduated college because he was with me in those beginning stages that he would do his homework and then he would help me with mine.

Life in a poor El Salvadoran village did not offer much hope for the future. Gangs, poverty, marriage and children at a young age, and working for low wages as a laborer were destined for Darwin. Darwin's mother,

Genesis (a pseudonym to protect her from ICE), was increasingly concerned about life's limitations for her children and the long absences of her husband. When she learned about his marital infidelities, she realized she had to get out of the marriage and the nightmare of El Salvador and try to find a better life for her children. With the help of two brothers who lived in San Francisco, she made the agonizing decision to leave her family and make the dangerous trip to the States in 2005. Her brothers had sent her money to help pay the coyotes (smugglers) along the way.

Like so many others who fled El Salvador, she left to find a place that was safe and would allow her to rebuild her life and one day bring her children to a place where they would be given the opportunity to live in peace, get educated, and pursue their potential.

Mom made herself a promise that if she was going to leave El Salvador, she was going to leave for a purpose, and that purpose was us. At that time, we were four kids. Our last sister hadn't been born yet.

Genesis made the dangerous journey from El Salvador: weeks of walking, hiding, taking buses, running, and paying the coyotes for protection. Finally, she was able to cross from Mexico into the United States near San Diego. The trip cost a total of $7,000, which was funded by her brothers. She stayed in San Francisco with her brother and worked two jobs to save money to bring her family. She cleaned hotel rooms and washed dishes in restaurants. Several months later, she called Pedro and offered him another chance at a life together.

They hadn't talked in six to eight months. She called Dad and told him "Okay, I'll make you a deal. I forgive you and I'll pay for your trip to the U.S. and we can start living here in San Francisco, but you have to work your ass off to be able to bring the kids here."

Pedro too wanted to be in America with his family, so he took the same arduous trip to San Francisco to join Genesis. Darwin and his siblings stayed in their village and were taken care of by his grandmothers and extended family. About a year later, Darwin's youngest sister was born in San Francisco. Soon after, Darwin received the phone call that would change his life.

The Unwanted Phone Call from Dad

By this time, it was already April 2007 and that's when Dad called and said, "Okay, pack your things up, you guys are leaving tomorrow." And I always referred to that as the Unwanted Phone Call from Dad because you know as a twelve-year-old you don't want to leave your whole community, you don't want to leave your grandmas who you grew up with and even though I was beginning to understand what life in La Union would mean for me, I wanted to stay.

The call came on April 18, and without any chance to say goodbye to their friends, he and his brother were picked up by coyotes the next morning. The sisters stayed behind with the grandmothers. Darwin was twelve and Mario was eleven. The journey to Tijuana would take two weeks, and there they would make plans to cross the border.

It was tough, because I didn't know the Mexican way of life. I didn't know what tacos or burritos were, since that is not what we eat in El Salvador. I had to pretend I was Mexican. I needed to learn some Mexican history and symbols like the flag. I had to learn all of that to pass myself off as Mexican. I've always been that type of person who memorizes things because part of being blind is developing other senses, and I was able to learn. Mario would read to me and I would be memorizing stuff just in case the police in Mexico would stop us and ask us questions.

After successfully making it to Tijuana, he and Mario got separated from each other. Another coyote took Mario to Arizona, and Darwin remained in Tijuana. The coyotes then moved him to Mexicali. This was the beginning of a very painful chapter in Darwin's life.

Mexicali is very hot. I can handle heat, I come from heat, but it was nothing like Mexicali. We tried crossing the border at 1 P.M., right when that sun is highest. I was told to join a group of adults. I was the youngest of the eight people.

Since I was the least heavy, they wanted me to get on a man's back, climb the fence and then jump over. And I was like, "Sweet, I can do that." I'm not from the cities, so I was used to doing dangerous things at some point, getting up to the trees, even with my blindness. But the fence was high, and in the middle of the day the metal got so hot, and burned my hands just to touch it. At the top, I had to let go and just let myself drop and I twisted my ankle.

Immediately I saw the border security coming after us. I couldn't run, so I was caught and arrested along with the others. I was classified as an unaccompanied minor. I had no idea what that meant. I was taken to a detention center for minors. It is really a prison. Four other teens and I were placed in a secure cell with a heavy metal door that could only be opened from the outside. We were each given one blanket and slept on the concrete. The youngest child in our cell was four. We were not allowed out of the cell. The toilet was separated by a small wall.

Darwin was held there for five days. He knew that calling his parents would not be a good idea since it could lead to their deportation, so he contacted his uncle, a U.S. citizen, to update him and convey messages to his parents. He was then taken by plane with other minors to El Paso, Texas, for processing. It was there that he was reunited with his brother, who had also been arrested crossing the border. They were taken in by a family for about two months while the authorities tried to figure out what to do with them as they were unaccompanied minors. His dad asked a friend to file for his children's guardianship, as he could not. After a lengthy process, the friend was awarded guardianship and came to El Paso to get Darwin and Mario.

The Family Restored but Unprotected

On June 19, 2007, I was reunited with my parents in San Francisco. I was so happy to see mom and dad again. I felt fortunate to have them in my life. I was twelve, but I knew that many kids whose parents leave for the United States are often never reunited. It was cold in San Francisco that day, but seeing mom and dad again made me feel warm. I was a happy camper as you say here in America!

We lived right in the heart of Tenderloin, which is all my parents could afford even working two jobs each. We lived there for three years surrounded by prostitution, drugs, homeless and mentally ill people wandering the streets. Although we did not know English, Mario and I started middle school. We went to a school that was really designed for migrant children.

It was here that Darwin learned that as a person with disabilities he would be given special accommodations for learning.

They assigned someone from the district, Mr. Steve, I used to call him, to come to see me every Wednesday after school and teach me the neighborhood. He taught me how to cross the streets as a vision impaired person. He really helped me adjust to city life, which I had never experienced before. La Union had only dirt streets and no lights or signs. The city was 100 percent different from the way of life for a young kid coming from a village in El Salvador. Mr. Steve taught me how to take the trains and buses. He was one of those early supporters I had in America, who I'm extremely thankful for. He connected me with the Lighthouse for the Blind in San Francisco, and that's where I started making some connections.

It was Mr. Steve who got Darwin a CCTV (a machine that enlarges print) from the school district so that he could start reading. He helped Darwin learn the city in order to apply for the one-week camp that

Lighthouse runs each summer for young people and adults with vision disabilities.

It's called Enchanted Hills camp. The camp is fully accessible. I went there the summer between my seventh and eighth grade years. As soon as I arrived, I was told that no one spoke Spanish. So, it was a great place for me to practice my English and have fun. This was the first of many experiences where I really learned how to speak English.

Darwin's youngest sister, Sadie, was born in the United States in 2007, so she was automatically a citizen. But in the States, DACA was not enacted until 2012. So his parents faced a dilemma: return home to the place they knew and loved even though it was filled with gangs, corruption, violence, and poverty, or remain in the United States under the constant threat of deportation. They decided to stay, feeling America would be the best place to raise children, give them a good education, and provide for their family.

Except for my sister we were all undocumented. We were here illegally, which at that time meant no driver's licenses, nothing, not even identification. The only form of identification my parents had was their passport. Their El Salvadorian passport. They were always worried about being deported, but I think they had to stay positive because they worked, and were with many of their family. They also knew that San Francisco was a good place to live for someone who's in that situation.

When Darwin arrived in San Francisco, he had to go to an immigration hearing with his brother Mario and their guardian. They were told that they needed to return within six months with an attorney. But they could not afford one, and his family had no idea how to network with agencies that helped refugees with immigrant issues. By now Darwin was thirteen and Mario was twelve.

So, we go there, put on my headphones for translation and I hear the attorney on the other side. All professional and fancy in his suit and

everything. "We're advocating for Darwin Velasquez and Mario Velas-
quez to be deported immediately to El Salvador." And then the judge
said, "Well, I know your position, Counsel, but there's a process
here and the kids still have two more hearings for them to be able to
have an attorney." So, then the judge said to us, "You should bring an
attorney next time because it will really help you. Be sure to have
an attorney."

Darwin and Mario reported the news to their parents, who were at a
complete loss of what to do. They each had paid $7,000 to be brought to the
United States and now had no savings at all. So, the two boys returned to
court without an attorney and were warned by the judge that they had one
last chance to come with a legal advocate or else they would be deported.

Like so many other immigrants who had no access to funds or resources,
Darwin and Mario were not able to get the legal help they needed, so they
simply did not return to the courtroom, and instead lived illegally in the
United States. For four years, Darwin was on a list of people to be deported.
If he had been picked up for anything, he would have been sent back to El
Salvador. He remained in school. His parents moved out of the Tenderloin to a slightly better place, a garage converted to a tiny apartment in
the outer Mission. The neighborhood was safer, but the living conditions
were still very problematic with no heat and all the children in one room.

The Gifts of Sight and Higher Education

A year after he came to the States, Darwin went to a doctor at a free clinic,
who detected that he had a detached retina and needed a retina transplant.
The clinic did not require patients to be permanent residents. It found
donors who paid for his surgery, which was much more complex than
expected, and he needed several additional hours of anesthesia.

Mom told me that she thought that I was going to die, because in
recovery I never said a word, I never moved. But the doctor said, "Let's
keep waiting. If he doesn't wake up in three hours then we're going to

have to do something about it." And so, in the fourth hour that I wasn't waking up, they decided to bring me back to life with electric stimulation. That saved my life.

Darwin believes that his life has been saved several times: escaping El Salvador, crossing the border, and having the retina surgery. These trials made him stronger.

So, my senior year hit in 2012–2013, and I wanted to go to college. I got involved with a wonderful program called College Track. Every day after school, I would go to their office and do homework with the tutors because they would have the patience to teach me English or do some math problems with me one on one. At high school they just didn't have the capacity to do that. And they paid for thirteen college applications for me.

I didn't know what it meant to be undocumented. I was barely turning eighteen and I got rejected from every single university I applied to, because my math was horrible and my English was limited. I got rejected from every state school and the University of San Francisco. I still have that letter, framed. I'm going to keep it all together— the first rejection letter, the later acceptance letter, and the diploma—all together. I have been always competitive with myself, not with others, but with myself. I always expected big things for me. But this was not the best for me. I felt terrible.

I was so pissed off that I didn't get into any university that I wanted to go back to El Salvador. I had been told if you don't go to a four-year university, you're a loser. And you're really a loser if you go to community college. But my mentors who I met through College Track encouraged me to go to community college to become a more competitive student and reapply. They worked with me and my personal statements and my college applications.

They convinced me to go to Skyline Community College. They suggested that I enroll for a semester or a whole academic year and see if

*I like it. My mentor Tony Prest connected me with a few professors he
knew at Skyline.*

Darwin had met Tony at the beginning of his senior year of high school
through College Track. He connected Darwin to the Puente program,
which helps students succeed at community college and prepares them
academically for a four-year college. With DACA now in place, he could
go to college. He barely made the cutoff, as the program is for children
who came to the United States before the age of sixteen and who were in
the States by June 15, 2007. Darwin had arrived only one month earlier,
on May 10, 2007.

*And, I get in. I get to Skyline with my scheduled four classes that I was
going to take. I go there, and see that all the professors and students
are serious, and that this is real college. This is not for losers, this is
for people who really want it. It clicked for me that first day.*

*This is for hardworking people. Tony told me that if I was willing
to put in the work, to get my butt into studying, I'd be able to transfer
after two years. And so I did.*

Darwin learned quickly the demands of college life. He devoted all his
energies to succeeding. He viewed it as a full-time job. The Disabilities
Center at Skyline introduced him to the Kurzweil software program, which
reads the text out loud. It still took Darwin a lot longer to read, but this
program allowed him to compete with the other students. During his second semester at Skyline, he learned about its study-abroad program.
Thanks to DACA, which started in 2012, he now had an ID, a work permit, and the ability to apply for a permit to travel outside the country for
educational purposes.

*This was an opportunity I really wanted. I had not left the country since
I came as an unaccompanied minor. I applied and received notice that
I had been accepted to the study-abroad program for the first semester
of my second year. The study-abroad program at Skyline was a*

partnership between various community colleges in the Bay Area, with the American Institute of Foreign Study. They take their students to Paris, London, or Barcelona. During my semester, they were going to Paris.

The major problem was the tuition of $12,000. To make it happen, I worked several jobs and got scholarships. I told my parents that I was going to Paris to study abroad. My parents were worried. But I felt that this was my decision. This was my thing. I was going to do it. And if I failed, it was going to be my failure.

Darwin immersed himself in the Paris culture and in his learning. He had a crush on a girl who asked him if he wanted to go to Auschwitz with her during the break. He had no idea what it was. He only knew that he wanted to be with her.

There's something about Poland, especially being at Auschwitz that was really cold.

I was there for eight hours. I imagined the suffering for the people held there. By the end of the trip I completely forgot that I had a crush on her because it was such an amazing experience to not only have gone to study abroad in Paris, but to be able to see and experience evil the way I got to see everything and learn firsthand. That is the best kind of education.

Upon his return, he reapplied to USF. This time, he was admitted as he had done well at Skyline. He was given a generous scholarship at USF and also received a scholarship from College Track.

I describe the USF experience as going from Double A baseball to the big leagues. It's a huge change from community college. Much more demanding, much more reading. I loved the professors because they cared about my situation. It was a huge jump academically for me. I was so proud when I got all Bs my first semester. I worked nonstop to accomplish this.

At Skyline, I think the longest article I read was ten to fifteen pages. Now it was fifty- to sixty-page articles just for one class. That's huge! And then I had to be able to understand it and comprehend it and take my ideas and opinions and be able to participate in class. It took a lot.

During his senior year Darwin carried eighteen units a semester and worked thirty hours a week.

I worked at College Track, the same program that had benefited me. I saw it as an opportunity to give back. They wanted a full-time person. I explained my situation and said I would not be graduating until December 2017. They allowed me to work thirty hours a week so that I could get my diploma and begin full-time work with them two days after I graduated. We had many Dreamers. I was the organizational expert to assist our Dreamers to resolve their immigration matters. I also researched, edited and published a monthly newsletter with resources and updates for our Dreamers. I also ensured every DACA beneficiary who is part of College Track had their work permits reviewed and were in good order.

DACA and the Almost Impossible Road to Citizenship

Today Darwin is deeply appreciative of the opportunities that DACA has provided him, but like all other DACA beneficiaries, he knows that right now it is not a path to citizenship and that in the political climate of 2018, nothing is certain. He speaks about it openly as he feels it must be addressed openly and people must hear directly from people who entered the country without documents and why they did it.

It makes you nervous that, one, I could be deported at any time. Two, that my parents could be deported. The reason that I'm not fearful is because, if we don't put a face, if we don't put a voice, if we don't put words into this debate that's going on, if we just let the president speak without knowledge, without firsthand experience, then we're lacking the possibility of fighting for a permanent residency that I truly think we deserve.

And this is why. First, we were young when we came to this country and grew up here. Second, we pay taxes to this country. If you have DACA, you must pay taxes if you're employed. Over 90 percent of DACA beneficiaries are employed and therefore pay taxes. Third, it's not that this thing is just given to us. We must register with the government. We must provide our real names, real identities, real addresses. You must renew every two years and pay $495 each time to have a work permit.

Many people don't understand that most DACA beneficiaries grew up in this country. This country already invested in us by getting us through high school, getting support from a lot of organizations, giving us money to pursue a college or graduate education. It's not like we are unskilled, if you want to call it that. We have been educated in American schools and universities. We have studied with Americans who are either born here or permanent residents. We have studied with international students. We have been educated by American professors. It's not like we're different. Our only difference is our immigration status. We want to contribute fully to America.

Under DACA you cannot vote. You are not eligible for a pathway to citizenship, which means you're not eligible for a Green Card. You cannot have a credit card. In this country, credit runs the world as well as your life, right? Even to rent you need credit. We're not able to build our credit because we are not able to even take loans, federal student loans to pursue a college education. We must rely on scholarships or organizations that are willing to give money to us.

Before the current president attempted to terminate DACA, I could travel to El Salvador under three purposes: humanitarian, business or education. This is no longer under the new administration. I visited El Salvador five times. But now I am never safe going back. Meaning, traveling with a travel permit does not guarantee returning to the

United States. One time I almost got deported in error while I was going through customs at Bush Airport back in January of 2017.

The village is still very poor. Like I said, there are only three houses that have WIFI. A few houses have cable. There's the main street, with just hot pavement, or concrete over it. It's not even asphalt in it. But, that's an improvement compared to not having anything. They are starting to see street lighting, which is amazing. Now, they have at least a nurse and a doctor who go there once or twice a week to treat people. They're shooting to have a permanent nurse, and to open a clinic there.

Many of my friends have died from gang violence. I left at the age of twelve and many got recruited in their early teens. Friends that I would have never thought would join a gang, did. They were exposed to it, because that was the norm: to look cool, or to be cool. Other people are living in terrible poverty. For example, on one of my trips back home, I befriended this kid. He is very smart, and his mother left him, his dad left him, too, so he's living with the neighbors. It's not like here, where you don't know your neighbors' lives. Over there it's different. But he's living very poor. The family literally lives in a shack with carton boxes, little wooden houses.

So, I'm helping the kid to go to school. He's in fourth grade, and he thinks of me as a father figure. I feel that I already have my first son. Every year I send him money for school supplies and uniforms and shoes. From time to time, I send him money just to have a little extra. But, I'm using those incentives for him to go to school because I know that he's very sharp, and I know that if he dedicates himself and does not get into gangs, he has a bright future even though he's already nine. He's very smart. He's a very smart kid. I always tell him, "Don't get into gangs. You will always have my support. I know that you are only in fourth grade right now, but if you continue like that, I'm going to help you to get to university." So, I am happy to provide those little incentives for that kid to be able to go to school.

Darwin's parents are hardworking people with good jobs who pay their taxes but are not eligible for any benefits. They also have no medical insurance. Recently, Darwin's dad had to go to the ER and the visit cost around $10,000, which he will try to pay over time. They have no pathway to citizenship. They never take vacations. They have no desire to return to El Salvador and fear for their lives if they go back, but they have a backup plan if deported. They have secured land in their small village to build a house on. They would prefer to invest in their new home, the United States, but that is not possible.

> *They still identify culturally as Salvadorians, even though they love this country. I think they are very sad and they don't see any future for them obtaining legal residency at some point in the current political climate.*

Darwin is working full time and living with his El Salvadoran wife in an apartment. They are expecting their first child. He lives a "normal life" but always with the worry that he or his parents could be deported. His dad has been very ill and is unable to get needed medical attention. He has dreams of pursuing graduate school.

> *It's a dream maybe one day to come true. I want to go to law school at some point. But I love teaching, so I want to get my master's. I'm considering the School of Education, with a focus on Human Rights at USF. Also, that program is designed for working professionals.*

Darwin takes nothing for granted. He has accomplished so many goals because of his work ethic and his positive attitude. He is now adjusting to life in the full-time work world. He is deeply grateful to all those who have helped him and taken a chance to give him an opportunity.

> *So, I'm very glad that the company that I work for gave me a job, despite my vision impairment because that happens in the workforce, too. A lot of companies won't hire you if you have some sort of impairment because they think that you won't be productive at work. I'm glad that that company that I work for took a chance with me.*

Darwin is deeply appreciative of what the United States has afforded him, and his greatest desire is to give back. He takes full responsibility for his life and does not let his visual impairment interfere with his goals. He is willing to work very hard. He has many dreams of higher education, of buying a house, and of becoming a U.S. citizen so that he can vote and fully participate in the democracy. He also points out that the battle for citizenship will never be won without the support of many more Americans, especially leaders.

> I think that this needs to be not just a movement for the undocumented. It has to be supported by U.S. citizens. University presidents, teachers, professionals, working-class people, everyone needs to be involved. I think university leaders and professors should do more. Not just public statements. Not just declaring your campus sanctuary. If ICE wants to go to a university, they will go, because they have federal authority. Right now, we don't have sufficient support outside our own community. We need more support from lawyers, from intergovernmental agencies.

However, his fate is not in his own hands. Like all other Dreamers, he lives a precarious life, not knowing what political decision could lead to deportation. He simply wants to live a safe life with opportunity for growth and fulfillment. He is profoundly sad that his home country has fallen into ruin and cannot afford him those opportunities. This is not the life he envisioned, but it is the life he fully embraces.

Although his sight is limited, his vision is clear. He knows what he wants, and if he is given the opportunity to do it, he will be one more immigrant that greatly enriches American life.

CHAPTER 9

KIEN HA QUACH

VIETNAM

When we returned to Vietnam many years after the war, my son, Dan-iel, was able to reconnect with his roots and have a better under-standing of his family's history. He could see the country through my eyes. Saigon had become very different than the Saigon of my memo-ries. Now there was chaos. Then there was culture and family.

Kien Ha Quach is calm and composed as we sit talking in the outside garden. She has lived in Oklahoma City, Oklahoma, for over thirty-five years. She looks much younger than her eighty years. Her face does not show the anguish of her life and all that she left behind in Vietnam.

Vietnamese refugees represent the sixth-largest immigrant group in the United States. Vietnamese migration in large numbers (230,000 by 1980 and many more to come later) began after the Vietnam War in 1975. The Viet-nam War represents one of the most painful episodes of American history. It was a time of division and conflict in America, with the government com-mitted to stopping communism from spreading in Southeast Asia, while most Americans were vehemently opposed to U.S. involvement in the war.

The roots of the Vietnam War lie in the 1954 Geneva Accords, which divided Vietnam along the 17th Parallel into North Vietnam and South Vietnam. While North Vietnam was controlled by communist Viet Minh forces led by Ho Chi Minh, the United States supported anti-communist politician Ngo Dinh Diem and South Vietnam's government. By 1964, the United States believed that increasing its military presence in the region was the only solution to stop the spread of communism.

It was not until January 1973 that the United States and North Vietnam finalized a peace agreement. War continued between North Vietnam and South Vietnam until April 30, 1975, when Saigon was captured by the North and renamed Ho Chi Minh City. Vietnam was finally unified in 1976 as the Socialist Republic of Vietnam. Retribution by the new government against those who had fought the North during the war threatened the human rights of South Vietnamese residents. Forced relocation, imprisonment, and executions were standard. Many were sent to prison camps and approximately 65,000 were executed.

The war took a large toll on the American people. There were over 58,000 military deaths, hundreds of thousands injured, and many who came home suffering from post-traumatic stress disorder. That the United States lost the war had a demoralizing impact on the American psyche. The feeling that this was a war that America should have never entered, the agony of losing so many people, and the guilt of the ravaging impact the United States had in Southeast Asia all contributed to an increase in the humanitarian impulse to help refugees from South Vietnam.

The war also took a huge toll on the Vietnamese people. An estimated 2 million were killed, 3 million were wounded, and 12 million became refugees. The infrastructure of the country was destroyed. The United States played a key role in helping people relocate. In 1975, about 125,000 Vietnamese refugees arrived in the United States via a U.S.-sponsored evacuation program following the end of the Vietnam War. From 1976 to 1977, the number of refugee arrivals dropped sharply for the most part because the United States denied admission to Vietnamese individuals except for family reunification. However, the more the American people learned about the number of refugees, the more they put pressure on the State Department to increase immigration quotas from Vietnam. The years of mass exodus were 1978–1979, with many, like Kien and her family, leaving on poorly constructed boats (approximately 800,000 people). This led to the label of "boat people." An estimated one-third of them died while making the trip.

> For refugees, it will be very difficult when you first arrive here, but over time things will get better. The most important thing I have learned is that you have to help people when you can. The struggles here are always difficult at the beginning, but with time it gets better if you're willing to work, and work hard.

THE LIFE BEFORE AND THE LIFE AFTER

This was the first time in thirty-seven years that anyone really asked me about my story and I am very grateful to be able to tell it. I still love the Vietnam I knew as a youth, the simplicity, the beauty, my family, the way of life. But over time, I have come to love the life that I have found here in America.

A Prosperous Early Childhood

Kien was born in 1938 in the village of Nam Dinh, in what was North Vietnam. Although she has lived in Oklahoma City since 1982, she still speaks only Vietnamese. Her son Daniel, a successful businessman, is her youngest child. Born in 1975, married with two young daughters, he is digesting his mother's story, some of which he did not know before, or perhaps he was too young to remember. He is helping draw the story out of her—a story that has never been shared outside of the family. Even the family has heard only parts of it. Daniel served as her translator for this interview, and the words below are hers.

My grandfather emigrated from China to Vietnam as a young boy. The French were powerful during that time. But my grandfather was able to grow up to become an entrepreneur. He owned a couple of shops and a hotel that catered to the French army. So, as a young girl growing up in Nam Dinh, my family had money and we had a good life.

We lived in a three-story private home. Although my sister and I shared a room and my two brothers shared another, we were considered upper-middle class by the standards of the day. My father, Quach Chau Thanh, eventually ran the hotel, and my mother, like nearly all other wealthy Vietnamese women of the time, took care of the family and the house. She was considered part of the aristocracy. My brothers attended school, but my sister and I were home schooled. It was not like today. Girls learned only French and domestic duties, like cooking, darning and sewing, so that we would have the skills to help in the house and for one day to raise families of our own.

But in 1953, when Kien was fifteen, life as she knew it ended when the Communists completed their takeover of North Vietnam. Ho Chi Minh had declared independence for the Democratic Republic of Vietnam (what was called North Vietnam) from France in 1945. Over the next eight years, during the first Indochina War, the Chinese communists supported Ho Chi Minh, and the United States supported France and the anti-communist Vietnamese forces. Ho Chi Minh's victory was the beginning of the end for Kien's idyllic childhood.

The War Intercedes and a Family Struggles

The Communists took over our hotel. That's when my family fled to the south. We left the home and the hotel my family had known for generations, and went to Hai Phong and eventually to Saigon. We each took only one bag and got into a large truck with others fleeing from the North. My grandmother refused to leave at first, as she did not want to leave behind her home and possessions. But we pleaded with her, telling her that the Communists would kill anyone of wealth who stayed behind, and she decided to join the family.

My father had brought money of different currencies, but quickly learned that the money we used in the north had no value in Saigon. Our only means for living, the money that my father brought, wasn't usable. So we moved in with an uncle. And my father got a job as an attendant at a car garage, checking people in and out, and earning very minimal wages. Yes, our lives changed when we moved. When we got to Saigon, we were just making ends meet. Life became more about just surviving.

Kien was one of nearly 1 million people who had fled the North and settled in Saigon, which had a population of about 5 million in the mid-1950s. Kien needed to find a job to help support her family.

And so, when I was eighteen, I went to work at a pharmacy. Every day I would take the bus and out the window I would often see a young man on a motorbike. The man would see me at the bus stop and I suppose I caught his attention. One day he stopped and spoke to me, and then started taking me home from work on his motorbike. This went on for a few years and transformed into a courtship. However, there was a big problem: the man, Ha Minh Hai, was Catholic and I was Buddhist. My parents were very upset about this and when we announced that we would be married, my father refused to attend the wedding, which was very painful. In those days, the woman converted to the man's religion, and so, I got baptized and converted. We were married in a Catholic church in Saigon in 1962 when I was twenty-four years old and Hai was twenty-six. It was a large wedding with many people attending and celebrating. There was a suckling pig and a variety of other foods for people to feast on at each table.

After the wedding we moved into the same apartment building that my husband's mother owned. It was a block long, and Hai's sister also lived there. Hai worked at a company that repaired planes after diagnosing the problem with X-ray technology. I had left the pharmacy, and was busy with the duties as a wife taking care of the home. In 1964, our first daughter, Lan, was born. It was then that my father reconciled with me and met his granddaughter. I had six more children in the next ten years.

My life was my family. In Saigon, there was no washing machine, and we used cloth diapers. All meals were eaten at home. The children went to Catholic school. I think the war, during that time in the city, did not have a big effect on us. My life was home, women did not discuss politics, so I didn't really know what was going on.

But during those years, my older brother died in an accident, and my younger brother escaped to Cambodia.

On April 30, 1975, Saigon fell to the Vietcong. Life changed again. There was less work available, and now Kien prepared food at home and sold it as a street vendor. She would go to the countryside to buy meat and rice for lower prices, then resell them in the market to make a small profit to help support her family. After Daniel's birth, she was working so hard that she had a miscarriage.

Dangerous Departure

A few years later as things were getting more volatile, her family began to explore ways to escape. The government was drafting teenagers to fight in Cambodia, and one of their best friends had lost a son. Lan was already fourteen and when she turned sixteen she would have to go into the army. The plan was to go by boat, and that required money to pay the smugglers. That was the only way out. Kien and Hai saved all their money, acquired by hard work, for the future of their seven children.

In June 1979, we planned our flight for the refugee camp of Kuala Bidong in Malaysia. We first waited ten days while the boat was being prepared and supplies were being gathered. Then, as soon as the sun had set, everyone walked across a swamp to the boat.

What should have been a three-day journey took over a month. The boat was not big, but it left with 108 passengers. It would arrive with only 106. Two would die along the way.

On the second day at sea, a hurricane hit, and the oil and water were washed off the boat. We had to return to Vietnam to purchase more supplies and pay more bribes to corrupt officials and smugglers. Several days later, we left and again ran into hurricanes.

The small boat was crammed with people. We kept running out of food and water, returning to Vietnam and bribing soldiers to get more supplies. The boat was raided three times by pirates. The raids were violent. They stole anything they found. All of my valuables, pictures

and personal things were taken. Hai, who was in ailing health, was
afraid the pirates would rape us so he put dirt all over my face and
the faces of our daughters, to make us look as unattractive as possi-
ble. The pirates took Hai's medicine.

Finally, we arrived at a small island in Malaysia, which I called
"Coconut Island," because its coconuts provided us with food and
water, and helped us survive. We slept on the coconut leaves on the
sand. Because we did not want to leave the island and get shipped
back, we sunk our boat. The Malaysian police came and beat many
people when they saw that we had no way to leave. Everyone was really
afraid. We gave the police whatever jewels or anything we had and
then they left.

Tragedy at Sea

A few days later, a French doctor came and helped treat the sick. But
my husband's condition had worsened. The doctor couldn't do any-
thing to help him, but he would go back to Pulau Bidong, another
small Malaysian island, and report to them that there were survivors
on this island who were stranded and needed help. He arranged for a
U.S. ship to get us. But this took several weeks. The ship was too large
to get close to the island, so we had to take smaller boats to get every-
one to the ship. My husband died on one of those little boats, and even
today I remember the exact date and time: it was at 10:15 P.M. on
August 9th, 1979. We had to hold our grief and cry in silent since we
didn't know how long the journey would take and we worried that they
would throw my husband's body into the sea.

As she told this part of the story, her eyes welled with tears and she
showed me her husband's photograph. She was reliving that day and the
tragedy of her husband's death. Although it had happened nearly forty
years ago, it was like it had just occurred. Kien's life changed at that moment
as she now had seven children on her own. She has never remarried.

The rest of the family was taken to the refugee camp on Bidong Island. This camp opened in 1978 to help deal with the growing number of people fleeing by boat. The camp's capacity was 4,500, but by the time they arrived the population had grown to about 45,000 in an area not much larger than a football field. Many called it "Hell Isle."

We stayed at the crowded refugee camp for about three months. We lived mostly on rice. But once a week they would come and give each family a chicken and canned sardines, and maybe some type of vegetable. I spent most of the day keeping the fire going to cook rice.

As with all refugee camps, there was tremendous chaos. Representatives from different countries tried to help resettle these refugees.

We were there for several months. But many countries were willing to sponsor my family, I think because I had so tragically lost my husband at sea and had seven young children. Ultimately, we chose Oklahoma because I had cousins there. We had to have physical exams and X-rays to screen for tuberculosis. What happened was during the process, my mother's X-rays and mine were stolen and switched with people who had the disease. So we were quarantined for a month. My seven children, and the rest of the family, went to America without me.

Making a Life in America

In early February 1980, the family took a ship to Hong Kong, then flew to San Francisco and on to Oklahoma City, where they were put in a small house temporarily. When Kien finally arrived a few months later, they rented a one-bedroom house in the northwest part of the city, near the Vietnamese community, with no air conditioning or heat, for $250 a month. They lived there for about a year, all sleeping on one mattress until finally someone got them help with federal housing. They moved to the projects on the northeast side of town, where everyone else was African American.

*Our new apartment was much more spacious than we had. We had
two floors. There were actually five rooms, five separate rooms. We
lived on $800 a month, which was very small for so many people.
Daniel's friend David Glover and his family, which was also very
poor, extended the hand of friendship to us and gave our family
clothes. I did my best to take care of my children. The children all
went to school in the projects and never experienced any discrimination. They were accepted for who they were. That first year, there was
a period when I couldn't pay the gas bill. I brought it to the Catholic
Church, and they paid it. We were living on a very tight, tight budget.
I would watch for a sale on chicken or whatever and stock up on it,
put it in the freezer. Years later I got a job working the night shift in
a candy factory, making minimum wage of $3.50 an hour. I was
required to carry heavy trays and you see that I am a petite woman.
I broke my wrist and had to go on disability.*

They spent a decade in this tiny apartment, but clearly Kien's children
emerged from that part of their lives instilled with a deep appreciation of
family and friendship, and the importance of generosity and education.

*When my oldest son graduated from the University of Oklahoma as
an engineer, we were able to relocate to the other side of the city to a
three-bedroom, two-bath house with a backyard in a less segregated,
lower-middle-class neighborhood. This was a major step up from the
apartment. All of my children graduated from the university except
for my oldest daughter. They did this by working, and getting scholarships and loans. Education is very important for me, especially
because I never had one. I wanted my children to do better and knew
that education was the key to moving ahead.*

Kien's children are now all grown with families of their own living in
Oklahoma City, Texas, and California. They work as pharmacists and busi-
nesspeople, and one is an engineer. She has twelve grandchildren and

two great-grandchildren. Kien lives with her oldest granddaughter in a very comfortable home. Her passion is her garden; she is a master gardener. It is filled with vegetables, plants, and flowers. The garden is a lens into Kien's life: it has a graceful aesthetic, filled with beauty and lovingly nurtured. Besides working on her garden, Kien enjoys watching Korean drama and cooking videos on YouTube. Holding tightly to her rosary, she prays daily for her family's health and well-being. Kien has a very strong faith.

She is deeply grateful for being here in America, knowing that this life would never have been possible in Vietnam.

> *I appreciate being an American because of the opportunities. I appreciate the grants and scholarships my children received to go to college. I appreciate the social security benefits I've received since I was sixty-five. If we had been in Vietnam, for six of my children to have gone to university and become a pharmacist, an engineer, a couple of businesspeople, I would have had to come from a great means of wealth. Otherwise that would not have been possible.*

A Visit Home to Vietnam

In 2009, Daniel organized a trip to take Kien back to Vietnam for the first time. It had been thirty years since the perilous boat ride fleeing their home. They planned to spend the Chinese New Year there to celebrate with the family who remained there. But Kien had not let anyone know they were coming as she did not want to impose on them. However, she had a few of the addresses of family members with her. In Ho Chi Minh City (formerly Saigon), they took a taxi to one of the homes where her sister-in-law lived, which had once been the house of her grandmother. The house showed its age and the toll of the war. Daniel got to see his birthplace, right next door. For Kien it was a deeply moving journey.

> *For me, it was a very emotional visit. Not only to be back home, or to see relatives we had not seen in so many years, but because when we left Vietnam, I had also left behind the part of my life with my*

husband. There was life before the loss of my husband, and there was
a very different life after.

What a journey Kien has been through, starting in her hometown of
Nam Dinh, to Hai Phong, to Saigon, to the boat on the open seas and the
refugee camp in Malaysia. Ultimately, she came to Oklahoma City in
the middle of America and raised seven children on her own.

I got my strength from the miracle of my faith. I pray to Mother Mary
and God. Years ago, I was very sick, but my prayers gave me the
strength to go on with life.

Daniel explains what he has learned from his mom. "She's an inspira-
tion because of her strength. For any single person to endure so much pain
and suffering and sacrifice, I think about my mom. I think about her self-
lessness and putting her family, our needs, above hers."

At her eightieth birthday, the entire family gathered around her. She
had prepared her remarks for this very special occasion. Her eyes spar-
kled with joy as she expressed how grateful she is to have such a wonderful family. Looking at the extended family surrounding her, it was clear
that Kien, through her courage and tenacity, has given so many gifts to
her children that enrich the fabric of American life.

CHAPTER 10

WILITA SANGUMA

DEMOCRATIC REPUBLIC OF CONGO (DRC)

*I survived. Yes, I saw things and experienced things and got a bunch
of different injuries from trying to escape. But I think seeing that horror was what really got to me, really changed my perception of the
world, I would say not in a positive way. That beautiful Congo I knew
went away and this wasn't the Congo that I knew anymore.*

Wilita Dennis-Park Sanguma, now a citizen with a family and a good job
in the United States, holds on to his memories of a peaceful childhood.
But the history of the Democratic Republic of Congo (DRC), formerly
known as Zaire, is one of brutal colonization, economic exploitation, famine and disease, and endless bloodshed. The world seems to have little
awareness of the amount of death and suffering that has taken place in
the DRC.

The geopolitical situation in the DRC has largely been dictated by the
events and actions of its neighbors Rwanda and Uganda. Initially, the violence that consumed Zaire in the 1990s was primarily a by-product of the
genocide that was occurring in Rwanda. An estimated 2 million Hutus fled
Rwanda following the victory of the Rwandan Patriotic Front (RPF) to
escape potential retribution by the Tutsis, and many of them settled in
Zaire. They began launching military incursions into Rwanda. These
attacks prompted a military invasion led by Rwanda that became known
as the First Congo War. The war devastated the country and resulted in
hundreds of thousands of deaths. Rwanda and its allies overthrew the government of Mobutu Sésé Seko and installed a new government led by
Laurent-Désiré Kabila.

The new government renamed the country the Democratic Republic of
Congo. Tensions continued to rise, and Kabila's government expelled
Rwandan and Ugandan forces from the DRC. This event was one of the
precipitating causes of the Second Congo War, which broke out in 1998.
The Second Congo War is also sometimes referred to as the African World
War. Nine African countries fought or contributed to the conflict, and

roughly twenty rebel groups (the most infamous being the Lord's Resistance Army) engaged in the bloodshed. Moreover, the war devastated the country and became the deadliest conflict worldwide since World War II. The violence, famine, disease, and destruction have claimed the lives of 6 million people and displaced more than 2 million people since 1998. It is estimated that 45,000 people (mostly young children) die every month in the DRC owing to the devastation of the past decade.

Things have somewhat stabilized in the DRC, but the country is still riddled with political corruption, human rights violations, violence, and the stripping of its vast mineral reserves by other nations.

There is great potential for the Congo. The major challenge is stabilizing the country so that the people can benefit from their indigenous wealth. Wilita remains deeply committed to shaping a Congo where people can live in peace.

My long-term goal is to create an organization that works with youth, a holistic program that gives them life, educational and peace-building skills. If it is effective it could spread from the Congo to other countries that have been torn apart. It is the youth who acquire the tools and the power to break the cycle of what has been in the past. We don't have to live the way our parents lived. We don't have to treat people the way they were treated. I think there are different ways of living, working and relating to people that can lead to a better way of life.

They Bombed My Church on Christmas Day

My childhood memories are very important to me especially when I think of the nightmare today. My memories ground me and give me hope. The people, the hospitality, the community, made it almost seem like a utopia. We had hardly anything, but you knew everyone in the community. You could, at a young age, walk around whatever time you want and not worry about anything dangerous because everyone knew you and your family.

A Childhood All Too Brief

Wilita grew up in Ipok, a small village near the city of Gemena in the northwest region of the DRC. But he was born in Chicago, making him a U.S. citizen, which would save his life one day.

In the late 1980s, Wilita's parents and three older siblings moved from the DRC to Chicago while his father, Mossai, studied at North Park University. When Wilita was just six months old, his parents took the family back to the DRC, where his father would continue to serve as a minister.

His father had a deep commitment to education. Wilita started studying at a young age. By the time he was in second grade, he and his friends would walk to Gemena, about two hours each way, to continue their education. They had few books but many rules.

The school was very strict in an old school type of way. If you did anything wrong, they sent you to the principal, then you had some whooping. The structure was from the time that the Congo was colonized so we kind of took on the Belgium school system.

His native language was Lingala. At home he spoke Mbaka, his mother tongue, and in school French was spoken. So at an early age Wilita was fluent in three languages. The two-hour walk home from school would often turn into a four-hour adventure.

Wilita and his friends could grab a snack off the abundant fruit trees, play soccer in the road, or walk into a market where relatives who were selling goods gave them free food. Some days, they would go down to the river to swim.

Not everything was easy. Wilita suffered from frequent bouts of malaria. One time, he almost died as he was taken by motorcycle to the nearest place for treatment, about fifty miles away.

But we began to understand that something was going on in the country, with the military. When you're younger, like ten years old, you're very intuitive and you listen to everything and you understand everything that's going on even though your parents might not tell you. I would listen to the radio and also got information from just listening to my parents conversing. I was able to pick up a lot of the things that were going on. But nothing was happening at the time that we could see or experience.

One day there was a clash that forced us to evacuate our home because something was happening nearby. We ran to the jungle and when we got the news that everything was cleared, we went back home. When we returned, we found our house that had been completely looted and we were forced to start over.

Life really changed on Christmas Day in 1998. My dad had recently gone back to the Fuller Seminary in the States to get his PhD in theology, so it was just my mom, my siblings and me. It was really unfortunate for anything to change on that particular day and I don't think I can ever forget it. Most of the population of the Congo are Christians and so on Christmas you dressed in your Sunday best and went to church. All day, from nine to three or even four. Church is part of the culture all year but on that day it's a really big celebration and almost everyone is singing and dancing and worshiping, so it's really beautiful. After the singing and dancing, the preacher was about to come and preach, and we heard this buzzing noise outside.

Nobody seemed particularly concerned; they lived in a no-fly zone, after all. Then there was a tremendous boom. The next thing Wilita knew, he and a friend were down on the ground. Time slowed as a surreal feeling enveloped Wilita. What seemed like a half hour on the ground was probably more like a few seconds.

> We were all freaking out, not knowing what was going on, and all I could see was the panic on people's faces. We started crawling underneath the pews in the church. I remember being stepped on, but we just kept crawling till we finally got outside. There was a ditch to the left of the church and I really thought I was going to die because everyone was stepping on us, and we almost got pushed into the hole.

That was the day his childhood, life as he knew it, ended abruptly. Everyone ran or crawled out of the church. No one knew what to do. Soon, he lost track of his friend. Terrorized, he began running, wondering where his mom and siblings were. He hid behind a palm tree near the church.

The bomb had hit about fifty yards away, and few people in Wilita's church were hurt because they had still been inside. The church nearby suffered the worst of the bombing. People had been outside when the bomb dropped, and many were killed.

> Unfortunately, we could see the remnants of the individuals as we went back to the main road, with the body parts, the arms swelled up. The amputations and casualties were everywhere.
>
> Growing up, and my mother will tell you this, I was a very hard-headed kid, so I never really cried. No matter what, even if I got hurt I always held it inside, but no one was around and it was just a really scary scene, so I started crying because I did not know what was happening. Then I started seeing people. Finally I found my family and we were able to congregate together. I remember everyone praying and my mum would tell you this too: She saw the tears streaming down my face and that was the first time she really saw me crying.

For me, from a really beautiful celebratory day to kind of the worst nightmare that you could possibly imagine, that was my exposure to the world. It was boom, this is reality right now and this is life right now and this is the Congo that you grew up in, this is reality right now.

The Sky Turned Red

Wilita stayed with his family in Gemena for a week, until the bombs started falling regularly. Every time they heard a plane, no matter what they were doing—cooking, eating, studying, praying—they would run and take cover. As the bombings intensified, Wilita's mom, Sabuli, decided that they had to get out, or they would be killed. She would rather die trying something, anything, than just sitting around. She woke the kids in the middle of the night and ordered them to pack up their belongings. They were going to flee the city.

They started walking alone in the dark but were joined by many others in the course of their journey.

From that young age, it seemed like there was thousands and thousands of people because everywhere I looked there were people. There were kids crying, there were people carrying the elderly and people that were hurt from the bombings or the fighting. There was just this mass exodus, so we felt we weren't alone at that moment. We walked and walked all night, and basically half of the next day, until we stopped at this one village.

In that village of only ten huts in the middle of the jungle there was a man who recognized my mum in the crowd and he said, "Oh, I'm an old friend of your husband's. We studied back in the days when he was younger." This guy who we don't know well offered us his home with his family until the fighting went away. We were so tired, had walked such a long way, and had nowhere to go except much farther. So we stayed there about a month. I don't remember the man's name,

and he didn't become a close family friend, he was just a guy who took
us in. He was a man who took us in with his family.

During the quiet of the day, they helped with farming and other tasks
to make sure there was enough food. However, the nights were long and
loud from the machine guns and rockets.

Every night it just got louder and louder because they got closer and
closer to us. The war got closer and closer. We felt we were really in
the middle of it. My mother again, did not want to sit there again, and
just be consumed by the fighting and just die, passively. So on a night
that was not too crazy we were going to try and make our way back
to Gemena from where we just escaped and try to actually leave the
country permanently.

Wilita credits his mother's courage, wisdom, and strength for their survival. She knew they had to keep moving. It was a long walk back, con-
tinually interrupted by hiding in the bushes when they heard a vehicle
approaching. This time they were alone on the road and finally got to
Gemena safely.

His home village and Gemena were under the horrific rule of many rebel
militias from Sudan and especially of Jean-Pierre Bemba. (Many years later
he was convicted by the International Criminal Court of crimes against
humanity.) He was a vicious leader who thought nothing of burning down
villages, raping women, and killing anyone who questioned his authority.
They had to try to escape this tyrannical leader who was one of the many
people responsible for murdering over 6 million people in the Congo.

Wilita's mom negotiated with a truck driver and gave him all their
money to take her and her five children out of the area. He had them pose
as his family. The truck was filled with sacks of corn and coffee. Wilita
and his family sat on top. Most roads were not paved, and the trip was very
dangerous. They were traveling to Zongo, near the border with the Central
African Republic (CAR). Under normal conditions the trip might take a

day, but this lasted longer than a week. As the days progressed, more people piled on top of the truck, including a soldier. Constant checkpoints caused delays. Every village and city had soldiers with machine guns stop all vehicles. Everyone was asked questions. Nobody knew what could happen with erratic, young soldiers.

At one checkpoint, when soldiers saw the soldier on the truck in a uniform they didn't know, they pulled him off, pointed their machine guns in our faces and yelled, "Who is this guy?" "What are you doing with him?" "Are you trying to help the enemy?" The angry soldiers said if we didn't identify the man we were all going to be killed. But we had no idea who he was.

I thought I was going to die that day. Then the soldier spoke up. He told them that he had forced himself on the truck and didn't know anyone else on it.

They started to interrogate him. There was a soldier standing right in front of him, pointing a gun right at his forehead. I can still see the man's eyes, bloodshot and red. He was sweating and shaking. The general then decided to let all us go and held him back.

Once we got on the truck and as we were leaving, we heard a gunshot and till this day I don't know if they shot the man or if they were just trying to scare us. From our other experiences, from what I'd seen, I think if they killed him it was probably the easiest and the best thing that could probably happen to him. The reason why I say that is because during our journey in all the different checkpoints, we saw a lot of things. Remnants of people left on the ground and in the river streams, some being eaten by pigs and dogs. That's what we saw almost every day, on the road and every time we stopped and I don't really know how we had an appetite, because we would stop somewhere to rest, and all around you were things that no one should ever see.

For us, you want to survive, you want to make it out, you want to live, so you're going to see it and just continue to persevere.

The journey continued with many more checkpoints. They had hidden their passports as the Congolese army did not want anyone leaving the country. At the last checkpoint before Zongo, the horror that took place was something Wilita would never be able to shake.

They saw a village, with people crying and screaming as smoke poured out of the houses. The huts were being burned down. Wilita saw whole families whose bodies were lying on the ground, burned beyond recognition.

At that moment, he recalled, he hated what people could do to one another. It filled him with despair. The nightmares never really went away. The smells, the sights, and the fear left an indelible mark.

These were families, these were people that were my grandparents' age, these were kids that were my age, these were kids that were my little brother's age. It's like a nightmare that's too real and you can't just overcome it by waking up.

I hated my country then and I didn't want anything to do with that country. It was like you have been told that the sky is blue all your life and out of nowhere it's like no, it's actually red.

Even today I can smell and see the ashes, falling and scattered. Even today, I can still put myself inside my nine-year-old body on the grass near the bushes hearing the people crying out. It's a powerful thing and I think in the Congo when people mourn, they mourn, they cry, and it almost sounds like they're singing a really sad song.

The journey continued but with two soldiers armed with machine guns atop the truck. They moved ahead in silence and fear before they finally reached Zongo.

Although it was illegal to leave the country, missionaries in the CAR urged them to flee as soon as possible. They were told to pretend that they were going fishing in the Bangui River. Early the next morning, Wilita's family set out in two boats. They arrived safely in the CAR. Missionaries, colleagues of his father's, were waiting for them. For the first time in two months, since the Christmas Day bombing, they felt safe.

> *The whole weight of the world just fell. It felt like we won the lottery. We escaped hell. It was a really joyous moment. And also we learned that we had the possibility of connecting with my father.*
>
> *Now we could call and he would know that we were alive. I remember celebrating, but I was crying tears of joy and sadness. We had escaped. But a lot of our family and relatives were still there, still hiding.*

They remained in the CAR for about a week until a special flight could be arranged to take them to Yaoundé, Cameroon. They stayed in Cameroon for three months while they began the application process for refugee status and for U.S. visas. Wilita did not have an American passport because he had been an infant when his family returned to the Congo. He also did not have a birth certificate. But his father was able to obtain proof of his birth in Chicago, and that allowed Wilita to get a visa. Had he not been born in the United States, had his father not been in the United States studying at that time, it is unknown whether the family would have been allowed in as refugees.

> *We probably would have just stayed in Yaoundé and Cameroon. And just lived there the rest of my life.*
>
> *But everything worked out and we got on this really big plane. We were going to France first. I remember, wow, everything is so fancy. Then when we got to France, they stopped us and they put us in what seemed like the airport jail. It was like a cell. And they started interrogating us. Asking a lot of questions. They took my brothers and sisters separately. And they asked them questions. And then they asked me questions separately as well. They also strip-searched everyone in the family too. We were held for more than sixteen hours.*

After the exhausting interrogation they boarded a plane for Los Angeles, where his father was waiting at the airport for them. In 1999, Wilita arrived in his birth country, a refugee from a nightmare in the country where his family had deep roots, not knowing a word of English. He had lived through so much horror. Now at ten years old he was about to start the next chapter of his life.

And the World Brightened

There was an apartment for us at Fuller Seminary. As we drove there through the city, I remember seeing all the big buildings and the cars. And they were in really good condition. And the lights were glaring from the cars and the way the light made the wheels look as they rolled, I knew that I was in a new kind of environment. I thought, This really is Heaven I guess. It was like I had skipped Hell and now I was in Heaven.

And so we got to our house and that's where we were able to stay for like a few years.

They arrived in the summer. Wilita and his siblings started being tutored in English. After a few years in elementary school and passing the English proficiency exam, he began middle school. It was not easy.

I was teased because of my heavy accent, for being African and the color of my skin, even though Pasadena is an ethnically diverse area. The schools were rough, with metal detectors, fights between different students and gang violence. There were racial slurs, name calling, making fun of me. But nothing they could say or did could hurt me as bad as what I escaped.

With everything Wilita had already been through, the problems in Pasadena did not bother him much. His athletic ability helped him integrate into American society. He was always the first chosen for football, soccer, and basketball because he was the fastest one there. He became popular and made many friends.

Sports created a niche and a haven for me. It was a place that I went to and I felt like everyone else. I felt respected. I felt loved. I felt like I was part of team. I think sports can do really good in this world, if we use it right.

In 2002, his father finished his doctorate at Fuller. One of the stipulations of his scholarship was that he would return to his home country to help the many people in need. His parents returned to the Congo, but they could not take Wilita with them. There was too great a threat of being captured and forced to become a child soldier. So they left the children, except his younger brother, in America, retaining their Green Card status. During his freshman year of high school in Pasadena, Wilita lived with one of his older sisters who was just beginning college. His siblings received visas and then Green Cards. Several years later they became citizens.

Wilita's father had formed close friendships with many people throughout the Fuller community. One family lived in Moraga in Northern California. Wilita barely knew them, but they knew he needed a family. They invited him to live with them and spend the next three years of high school at their home in an upper-middle-class, predominantly white suburb of San Francisco. The Breuls had three children of their own, all under the age of six, but they provided Wilita with shelter, food, love, and support. He attended an outstanding high school where he felt safe.

When we went out together as a family, people would look at us and wonder. They are white and they all had blond hair and here I was with them. And Moraga is not a very racially diverse community. But the Breul family helped to chip away at the hatred in my heart. They taught me again that the world could be bright. Without them, I would not be where I am today. Here was this family that offered to take on this child for three years, who they hardly knew, and had gone through a very traumatic experience. They took the risk to take me in. And they treated me like their own children.

Wilita flourished academically in high school. He starred on the soccer team and in track. His dream was to play collegiate soccer. But he broke his ankle in his senior year, ruining the chance of getting an athletic scholarship.

Wilita knew he could only go to a college where he might get some financial aid to help pay his tuition and living expenses. His parents, back in the Congo, barely had enough money for their own survival. In the fall of 2007, he enrolled at Fresno State. In 2009, he earned a scholarship to spend the fall semester studying in France. Upon his return, he declared a major in political science with a double minor in French and philosophy.

> At Fresno State, I majored in political science with an emphasis in international relations, but I loved philosophy and ethics. It was during that time that I was soul searching as well, and I think the classes and readings really helped me turn my heart. And from that point on, I was just really curious about why do we do things that we do? What is considered good? What is considered bad? And why?
>
> Meanwhile I was running track, which would help me be able to graduate in four years since I did not have money for more. Because when you were an athlete, you got to register first. Plus I wanted to prove to myself that I was capable of competing at a higher level and did not want to waste my potential since I was fortunate to be where I was there, given what I had been through.

In order to finish school in four years, Wilita took over twenty units a semester. Every summer, he held jobs ranging from an overnight stocker at Wal-Mart to working at the university as a conference and dorm supervisor.

Finding a Meaningful Life

It was at Fresno State that Wilita met his future wife, Brittany. She was friends with one of his friends, and they became part of the same crowd.

Over time, they became close. Wilita was so busy that he did not really think about entering into a relationship.

Brittany's background could not have been more different from Wilita's. She grew up in Temecula in Southern California, and her roots are Italian and Irish.

But with Brittany, it was one of those things that when you see some-thing really good in someone, then it's hard to just let that thing go away. And I think what attracted me most about her was the beauty in her heart.

Her parents were very loving and kind. The first time I came to visit was Thanksgiving, and they were very welcoming. I never thought that I was going to marry an American white person. I always thought I was going to marry an African. I think for me it was because cultur-ally that was what I was used to, and it's easier. Which is a danger-ous way of thinking, because then you get comfortable with your surroundings. You just stay in that realm.

Wilita graduated from Fresno State in 2011. He started a graduate pro-gram in international studies at the University of San Francisco (USF) that fall. Brittany had gotten into a graduate program in higher education there too. Through scholarships, loans, and jobs, Wilita managed to pay for the costly tuition. He worked at the University Ministry office, which covered room and board. At USF, Wilita was a well-respected person on campus.

I really want to be a good person, and I want to live my life that reflects the values of compassion and understanding. My key learning from all the work I did at University Ministry is the concept and practice of really intentionally examining your life and seeing all the different details that sometimes you will miss if you don't take the time to just sit back and reflect.

My studies focused on peace and conflict resolution. And again, I went back to why do people do what they do? I had spent years on my own reconciliation process and trying to accept what had happened to me in the Congo. For me, the questions were, How do you bring people together that had gone through such horrible reality? How do you really create something that's sustainable to make sure that something like that never happens again?

Wilita's thesis covered the peace-building process in the Congo. He examined the conflict, how the peace process unfolded, and why peace was not sustainable.

Why do peace agreements fail? Because they are conducted on the highest level by political leaders and not by the people who have lived through the conflict and suffered the most. Healing does not come from merely signing a peace treaty. That is just the beginning of a process that must take place between people and within oneself.

A Return Visit and with It, the Pain

In December 2011, Wilita returned to the Congo for the first time to visit his parents. They were living in Gemena, and he spent about a month there.

Right when I arrived at the airport, everything came back. The hatred, sadness. I walked around, I saw the chaos, all the soldiers, and the children selling peanuts on the streets. I wondered, Why aren't you in school, where you belong. You don't need to live like this. No one should live like this. The pain all came back, seeing the state of the country and how bad it still was.

But Wilita had a chance to see many relatives. He cried as he listened to their stories of how they were still living with death and pain all around them. On Christmas Day, he attended church with his family in Gemena. What had happened so many years before came rushing back to him. He did not want to be there. But he clutched his mother's hand and felt comforted.

He returned to the Congo again in the summer of 2012 to study the conflict between the Enyele and Munzaya tribes. He and a friend went to Dongo, which was still in conflict, to interview people for their perspective. During one of the interviews, soldiers approached and asked where he was from. He could not say the United States or they might hold him for ransom. Wilita said he was from another part of the Congo, Kinshasa. They accused him of being from the CAR. Terrified, Wilita wondered why he had come back and put himself in such danger. But the soldiers released him, and he immediately left the village to go back to Dongo.

On the way back, their motorbike broke down in the middle of the jungle. They pushed it to a nearby village where people had tools to fix it. The road they traveled on had been a killing field. Skulls and bones still littered the path, and Wilita worried that the people fixing the motorbike might have been some of the perpetrators. Eventually, they left and traveled through the night back to Dongo.

Filled with Dreams

Wilita earned his MA in December 2012. His career started at USF in the School of Management, where he helped develop its social justice initiatives and volunteerism. After a year and a half, he continued his work at University Ministries overseeing several volunteer and social justice programs. Wilita played a key role in many USF programs, bringing people together and teaching them through his own experiences.

Wilita and Brittany have been married since 2014 and have two children. Brittany created her own personalized wellness coaching company. In August 2017, Wilita started working with Summit Public Schools. With eleven schools in the Bay Area and the state of Washington, the organization helps prepare students for college and life based on a highly effective personalized learning model. It collaborates with public and charter schools to enhance the overall school environment.

As director of development, Wilita works with philanthropists and foundations to secure funding, especially for the Summit learning programs, which are offered for free. Wilita feels that his education has given him so many opportunities. He wants children to be given the same opportunity to obtain the skills and knowledge needed to pursue their dreams.

Youth is my passion. They need our attention. They need better schools and more learning opportunities for real growth.

Wilita and his family now live in Murrieta, California (about sixty miles from San Diego). It is a middle-class life. Wilita and Brittany want their daughters to experience the culture and richness of the Congo. And Wilita remains close to the Breul family, who had provided him with a home and an anchor during high school.

Wilita is filled with dreams of what he might do here or in the Congo. He hopes to create a holistic youth development program that addresses life skills and how to live as a good person in this world.

I believe that if given the right tools, if they learn about peace building, that perhaps young people will break the cycle of violence and oppression that we see everywhere in the world.

Because, before, when I lost hope in humanity, I thought life was very dark and no one, no country, cared for anyone. That's a horrible state of being. So, I see hope in people. I think as individuals we are capable of doing the most beautiful things and doing the ugliest things as well. I think if we were to have positive influences in our interactions with people, things can really turn around. If hatred can be learned and perpetuated, so can goodness.

I hope that I can inspire someone else and that I can create a few raindrops of goodness by the time that I leave this world. We want a community that is inclusive and connects to the issues of the real world.

I am the lucky one. I won the lottery, not of wealth, but of survival, freedom and opportunity many times.

CHAPTER 11

JAWAD KHAWARI

AFGHANISTAN

For the refugee, everything is lost behind. Our language, our family,
our friends, our education, our country. Because it is not the same as
here. People can go to university in Afghanistan and learn about law,
about engineering or medicine. Then they come here and work in a
warehouse, or drive a taxi. I am grateful to America, and the people
here are kind and helpful, but when you come here it feels like you
just lost everything you had and are born like a new person.

Jawad Khawari and his wife, Sadeqa, live in a sparse apartment in the
Little Kabul section of Sacramento, California, one of the country's largest centers of Afghan refugees. Jawad has been in this country for almost
two years, having survived war, harsh labor, combat, the Taliban, the
loss of home, and separation from family. His life is a reflection of Afghanistan's tumultuous history.

The area now known as Afghanistan has long seen foreign powers vying
for influence as it is a gateway between Asia and Europe. Since its incep-
tion as a modern state in the eighteenth century, Afghanistan has experienced profound economic and political instability. It was only during the
forty-year rule of King Zahir Shah that there was stability, but that came
to an end with a military coup in 1973. The new government established
close ties with the Soviet Union, but that was short-lived. Afghanistan has
been called the "Graveyard of Empires"—so many foreign powers have
tried to control the country, but none have lasted.

In December 1979, Soviet tanks stormed into Afghanistan. But there
was no quick victory. Instead, the war lasted nine years and cost an estimated 1–1.5 million civilian lives. According to the United Nations High
Commissioner for Refugees (UNHCR), the war also caused a huge
upheaval of Afghan people. Millions of Afghans fled to Iran and Pakistan.
The devastation and ensuing anarchy enabled the Taliban to rise to power,
which facilitated Afghanistan's evolution into a traditional Islamic state.
The Islamic Emirate of Afghanistan, as the country came to be known

under the Taliban's rule, further accentuated the refugee crisis. Many of the remaining intelligentsia fled Afghanistan to escape the purges of the new Taliban regime. Moreover, secularism was abolished and a fundamentalist Islamic state was established. The Taliban's emphasis on poppy cultivation to finance its military and the lack of any other significant source of revenue led to food and fuel shortages. It was widely reported that the food shortages were so severe that the country was on the verge of starvation.

The attacks on the United States on September 11, 2001, and the subsequent U.S.-led invasion, ushered in dramatic changes in Afghanistan, including a new era of instability. The invasion resulted in the Taliban's overthrow and the assumption of power of a Western-backed and democratically elected government. However, this upheaval exacerbated the internal displacement of Afghans and led to an uptick in people fleeing the country. The UNHCR estimates there are 1.2 million internally displaced people as well as more than 2.4 million refugees remaining in the region.

Thousands of Afghans have assisted U.S. and allied forces as translators or interpreters since 2001. In return for their service, the United States offered the possibility of qualifying for a Special Immigrant Visa. These Afghans faced a dire predicament. The Taliban threatened them and their families. With the chaos in U.S. immigration and refugee policy, the State Department has not honored many of the promises that were made to the Afghans who helped the troops. Many have waited for years and still have not received a visa.

In early 2019, 14,000 U.S. troops remained in Afghanistan working closely with Afghan military. (President Trump has announced that half will be withdrawn, but that plan has not yet been implemented.) Yet there seems to be little cessation of violence and terrorist attacks by the Taliban, which remains heavily funded by the sale of heroin to the rest of the world (it is estimated that 70–90 percent of the world's heroin originates in Afghanistan).

Afghanistan continues to be plagued by war, famine and poverty, and the growing opium epidemic. The United States has been there since 2001, and there is not any sign of stability in the country. In early 2019, the United States was negotiating with the Taliban about a withdrawal from Afghanistan. Even if the withdrawal occurs, it does not seem that this country plagued with problems will become any more stable. Thus, millions of people will continue to be displaced, and the refugee crisis will not abate.

I had dreamed of coming to the United States. And I got my dream. So I am not going to lose hope now. I survived civil war in Afghanistan, fleeing from my country to Iran and back again. I survived combat in the mountains, threats from the Taliban, long delays in getting a visa. Now my dream is to become an engineer, an educated, good man, to show that the Afghan people are not lazy. They lost their place, they want to be part of society, and want to do something better. When my children grow up, I have a story to tell them. "I survived, I came to the United States, I studied, and now I have something to say."

Empty Walls

Before I turned age thirty, I had moved so many times in my life, too many to count. I relied on people my father had to bribe, on friends who helped, on strangers who took us into their homes. Even today, living in the United States, I have never put one picture on our apartment walls. Because we will have to pay for the repairs when we have to move again one day.

Leaving Home for the First Time

Jawad's story began in 1988 in Bandar, a remote, mountainous village of 4,000 people in the Sang Takht district of Daykundi province, where he lived the first year of his life. There was no electricity or running water. Like all men in the village, his father, Qurban, was a farmer.

In 1989, when he was just one year old, Jawad's family fled Afghanistan and went to Iran.

At that time, the situation in my country was not good. Russia had attacked my country years before. The civil war was taking a tremendous toll. We were not safe. So we traveled into Iran as refugees. My parents, who shared the story with me, as I was too young to remember, found people who they paid to help us cross the border illegally. We walked for five days, day and night. Once past the border, other people were waiting to take us into Iran if we paid their price. It was a lot of money for my family. But they delivered all of us, including my brothers and sisters. We were not alone. There were about fifty families.

After crossing the border into Iran, they went to the city of Balochistan, near the border. Then after a month, they traveled to Mashad, where they oriented themselves to Iranian culture. They got new clothes, allowing them to better fit into their new life. After some months, they moved again to Tehran. Jawad's uncle, who lived in Tehran, made this possible. After staying with him for a month, they settled into their own place. In less than six months, they had left the simplicity of their home village to resettle right outside the large, bustling city of Tehran.

> We began our new life. My father worked as a farmer and my mother took care of the house, washing clothes and feeding the kids. There were now eight of us, plus my parents, living in a one-room apartment where we all slept on the floor. My first memory is when I was about the age of five, we were outside playing with the older kids. They were Irani and they were laughing at me because I could not speak as well as they did, because our language is a little different. We were speaking Dari. They spoke Farsi. But after a while, we became friends and I learned Farsi.
>
> I started school in the first grade. Nearby, there was an Afghani teacher who taught kids in his home. There were one hundred children ranging from first grade to fourth grade in the school. One blackboard and a small piece of chalk were the only supplies.

Over the years, they were able to move several times to better apartments from money earned by Jawad's older brothers. There were more rooms and they had beds. They slowly became more integrated into Iranian society. Jawad finally entered public school in the fifth grade, thanks to the relationships his family had made.

> The other children, who were Irani, were legal. So they would earn a certificate when they passed a grade. But they couldn't give me a certificate because I was illegal. They were kind and supported me and put me in school. They told me if I studied and worked hard, I would move up to the next grade. But it couldn't be official. They could not put my name on the certificate. Even though I was still struggling with the language and the differences in our cultures, I went to school through the eighth grade.

In 2003, after thirteen years in Iran, his family decided to return to Afghanistan. The United States had entered Afghanistan and the Taliban's brutal power had diminished. His parents felt it was safe to return. The Khawari family were considered refugees and were eligible for help from the UNHCR. It provided transportation to the border, a little food, and safe drinking water and gave each person a stipend for resettlement. Jawad's father decided they could not go back to their home village.

Returning to Afghanistan but Starting Over

We had lost everything. We had to start new life again. My father said that we must go to a city. That I must go to college, and study, so that I could make my own future. He felt strongly that if he took us back to our village, it would mean we all would become farmers. That is not what he wanted for us.

So we stayed in Herat, about ninety miles from the Iranian border. It was a big modern city. There were paved streets, there was electricity, water, a university. It looked like Iran, sharing the culture, trading back and forth.

But when we arrived we still did not have enough money to buy a good house or even build a house. So we were camping outside, on the ground. We had saved a little money from working in Iran and received a little more from the UNHCR. Each one of us received $300. We put it all together and we bought some land and my father and brothers and I started building our own home right there, in that place, from the ground up.

But after several months, we ran out of money. We stopped building, but we moved into that house. We couldn't buy a window. We couldn't buy a door. We couldn't buy a carpet. We just lived in there for a while and we started working different places, like in the market, in the bazaar. I couldn't go to school because I needed to get a job. I was fifteen at the time.

My father didn't force me. He told me, "Hey, Jawad, if you want,
there's a school. You can go to school." But, I could see the situation of
my family. I decided that I had to support them. I thought that in a
year or two, whenever we'd have enough money saved to set up every-
thing, I would go to school. So I worked outside in construction as a
laborer. Hard work. For two years. I rode five miles each way on my
bike to a place where workers would gather, waiting to be picked up
for a day job. My hands became rough, and during the night they
would really hurt, and I would put oil on them, making them a little
softer. I could then touch my face. I could pray. My hands helped me
not to cry.

In 2005, Jawad had the good fortune of finding a real job. A friend of
his helped get Jawad a job as a storekeeper working in the old city of Herat.
While working at the store, he met a young engineer named Jawad Khan,
who saw the potential in Jawad. He encouraged him to go back to school
and told him that learning English was critical to his future. This man
became a mentor to Jawad, and his company hired him. It also paid for
him to take English classes. Jawad's day then began at 5:00 A.M. He went
to English class from 6:00 to 7:00 A.M. and then would hurry home to get
to work by 8:00 A.M. In 2007, Jawad went to night school and in 2009 completed his high school education.

Over the years, Jawad learned about computers, drafting, and engineering. Although he was not an engineer, he took on more responsibility in
the company, Agha Khan Tours for Culture. He was then asked to move
back to Kabul and take on a major position with the company. He credits
a British man and one of the company's executives, Jolyon Leslie, who
believed in him and saw the great work he was doing and his leadership
skills. In his early twenties Jawad was promoted to managing director of
the office and was put in charge of about forty-five people. Many of the
engineers were angry to have such a young man who was not an engineer

as their manager. Despite the large responsibility, he made only $200 a month. The engineers were making $1,000 a month. But Jawad knew this was a great opportunity.

But as the project was coming to an end, Jolyon told Jawad that he needed to get more experience and he gave Jawad the first paid vacation of his life to find a new job where he could continue to grow. Jawad was initially angry as he felt he was being fired, but grew to understand that was not the case. This man wanted Jawad to get a university education and a degree so he could really advance.

After two weeks, one of my friends, who had become a translator with the U.S. military in Kandahar Province, suggested that I become a translator, too. My English was as good as his. We had been in the same class. I didn't have another job, and we could go together. But my parents felt that Kandahar was too dangerous. It was a war zone. I tried to explain to them that I had to go. Finally, they accepted it. I went to Kandahar—about a six-hour drive from Kehat.

My friend had made all the arrangements for me at the base, a camp with foreign people, who work with the U.S. military. They took my fingerprints. They did my background check. But I had to wait for a budge. So during the day, I went to find work in the city. It was dangerous because if the people find out you are going to work with the U.S. military, surely they are going to try to kill you. The city was filled with Taliban. You don't know who is connected to the Taliban, and who isn't, who are bad people, who are good. I could not share with anyone what I was doing. Once again I worked as a day laborer and had to keep making up stories about why I was there alone. I told them that I had lost my family. I just needed a little money. They believed me. I was very careful about my cell phone. I was worried that maybe the call was from the U.S. military. It was risky for me.

After a month, they called me and said I was hired.

High-Risk Work for the United States

My first assignment was for nine months. I did not go home during
that time, but I did call my parents, to tell them I was safe and working
with the U.S. military. After the first year, I was assigned another place,
in Zabul. It's close to the border of Pakistan. Very dangerous. But I
didn't tell my family. I told them I was working in the city. I was lying
to them.

In 2010, Jawad went out on combat missions with U.S. Special Forces
in a war-torn area near the Pakistan border. On one of the missions, his
vehicle was hit by an IED (improvised explosive device) and Jawad was
seriously injured. The gunner had been killed and the others were also
wounded. He was medevaced out on a Black Hawk helicopter and spent
about a month in Lagman hospital recovering from wounds in his legs and
a temporary loss of hearing. After recovering he was offered a desk job but
declined it because he felt a great loyalty to his friends in the Eighty-Second
Airborne. He wanted to continue serving on missions that were of critical importance.

In 2011, our platoon was transferred back to Kandahar. We created
checkpoints, made camp around the city of Kandahar. We screened
people every day on the road. We had meetings with the local people
about what was going on. It was interesting for me. I felt part of the
U.S. military. I had a uniform, helmet, everything. But I was not
authorized to go to some parts of the base and I did not have a gun.
Because we were local, they did not trust us fully.

After nine months, I traveled by airplane from Kandahar Airport
to Kabul, from Kabul to Herat. I stayed one month with my family. I
had made good money. I can say $8,000. Each month they paid me
$800 or $900. I saved it in my bank account and just gave it to my
family. But my family still didn't know that my work with the U.S.
military was much more than an office job.

*I was enjoying my work. I was speaking English with American sol-
diers. Some of us had become friends. I was asking them to tell me
about the United States. Tell me about where they were born. And they
told me about California. They told me about Texas. About Virginia.
I was imagining the United States. It was a dream for me.*

*Then one day in 2011, I was eating in the chow hall, and the lieu-
tenant of our team, an American named Rebecca Pember, who had
supported me and praised my work, asked me, "Hey, Jawad. Do you
want to go to the United States?" "What? Yes, of course!" I said. And
she said "Okay. There's a way. Just bring me your passport, your documents that prove you are Afghan, and I will talk to you." I couldn't
believe it.*

*I gathered everything and submitted it to her. She had written a
recommendation letter for me for a Special Immigration Visa (SIV),
and we sent everything through email. It would be a long process, but
it was the beginning.*

*In the meantime, the Taliban had found me through Facebook and
discovered that I was supporting the U.S. military. They sent a warning letter to my home. It said, "We found out your child, your boy, is
working with the U.S. military. He has to stop. He must back off." My
parents were seriously frightened for me. They insisted that I run away,
not back home, but to a different country. They knew I wouldn't be safe
at their home because the Taliban knew I might return there. They
were very angry with me. For lying to them and putting myself in danger. Sometimes when I called them, they wouldn't talk to me. And I
was worried for them, hoping and praying the Taliban wouldn't attack
them because of the work I was doing. I removed all photos from Facebook and lied on Facebook and to my parents about being in a new job.*

*Finally, on December 19, 2012, I got my visa interview at the U.S.
embassy in Kabul. They told me everything had been submitted and
I was done. I thought I was going to get my visa in 2013. I quit the job
with the military.*

The Long Wait for a Visa

Jawad relocated to Kabul. He used his skills working with Afghan people through the Chemonics Organization as a training specialist to prepare municipal employees for computer jobs. He was later sent to a remote village in the Daikundi province to help small municipalities guide construction projects. Each day he checked his email, eagerly awaiting news that he had been granted a Special Immigrant Visa. He could not call to check on his status, so every few months he would send an email. There was always the same response: "We don't know. We cannot estimate a time. We cannot guarantee that you will even get a visa. When your visa is approved, we will let you know."

This went on for over four years. He waited until 2016. He was frustrated and losing hope, and could not understand why others, who had not served in real combat missions, were getting visas.

He could not pursue his education in Afghanistan because he had no idea when he was leaving. His life was on hold, his destiny out of his hands. But his parents had other plans.

In the beginning of 2016, my parents decided, because they knew I had applied for a visa, that I should get married. They told me that they chose someone for me and wanted me to come home to meet her. Her name was Sadeqa and she was studying law at the university. If we liked each other, it would be made official. We would become engaged, have a party. But my parents insisted they were not forcing me to get married. This was part of the Afghan culture.

We met a few times at her house. We talked about our past, our future, about what was going on in our minds. What did I think about her? What did she think about me? Are we good for each other or not? After three visits, we agreed that we were a good match.

I was honest with her. I told her I was working with U.S. military. I had submitted my documents for a visa. I told her, if they granted

*me a visa, I would submit her documents, and she could come with
me as my wife. Otherwise, I would not go alone to the United States.
She agreed and said that wherever I go in the future, she will go with
me. We became engaged and had a small party of 200 people. Our
parents were happy.*

Jawad then submitted Sadeqa's documents to the U.S. embassy, saying
that she was his wife. They wanted to wait to have the real wedding party
until after a decision had been made about their fate. Jawad will never forget the email he received on June 16, 2016, congratulating him on being
granted a visa. Jawad and Sadeqa worked with the International Organization for Migration (IOM) to make all the arrangements for relocation,
as all they had were the Special Immigrant Visas. The IOM was established
in 1951 to help resettle refugees. However, like any other large organization,
it also had a process that requires patience.

*They asked us where we wanted to go. The only place where we knew
anyone was Sacramento, California, where many Afghani refugees
had resettled. On August 2, 2016, we received the news that we would
be leaving that month for America.*

*So just three weeks later we held a traditional Afghani wedding
where 2,000 people gathered to celebrate with us. Very few, besides our
families, knew that we would be leaving the country. Sadeqa wore a
dress filled with bright colors and detailed embroidery. People ate,
danced and celebrated until early in the morning.*

Once Again Making a New Life, This Time in America

*In the next few days, as we prepared for our departure on August 27, we
felt two different emotions. We were happy. We had just been married,
and we were starting a new life together. But we also felt sad, knowing
that we were leaving behind our families. Leaving our home. We were
going to a different country, where we had no friends, really, where we
had no family.*

On the day of our flight, Sadeqa's family and my family, and some of our friends, escorted us to the airport, and everyone was crying. It was a very sad moment. But, again, there were the two emotions at war with the other, because we were happy too. We were going to a good place. But we were feeling deep with loss. We were going far away and who knew when and if we would see our families again.

Jawad and Sadeqa flew from Herat to Kabul and then to Kuwait. Next was a seventeen-hour flight to Houston, where they went through U.S. customs. After that they flew to Denver and finally to Sacramento, where they arrived on August 29 exhausted and exhilarated, greeted by representatives of World Relief.

My life began again that day when we arrived in America. I had saved a thousand dollars, and the contents of a few suitcases was all we now had in the world. A woman greeted us with a smile and said, "Hi, I am Becca and I will be your case worker." She told us that they had not found a house for us yet, so they put us in a hotel. They paid for it. We were in the hotel for twenty-one days. And during this time, a family came to visit us, and they told us, "You can come to our house." But we knew it would be hard for them if we were going to go to their house. They had kids, and they probably did not have enough space.

But Kerry Ham, who is now the Sacramento office director of World Relief, gathered our luggage, and took us to his house in Roseville, which is near Sacramento. They invited us to stay until we had a house of our own and gave us a separate bedroom, shower, bathroom. We became friends with his family and his wife Sherri. We stayed there for eleven days.

They had volunteered to share their house with us. We understood the effort they were making. And we hadn't even known each other before. They just did it to help us.

In September 2016, our apartment, where we live today, was ready.
We have never put anything on the walls because we will have to pay
for the repairs when we move out one day.

After being set up by the generosity of World Relief, they lived on $350 in
food stamps and $500 a month from the Department of Human Assis-
tance. As Jawad's English was good, he secured a job within four months.
Along with many other Afghan and Iraqi refugees, he worked in an Apple
factory as a technician, fixing iPhones that were returned by customers.
He worked the evening shift from 4:00 P.M. to 12:30 A.M., making minimum wage ($12 an hour) but not receiving any benefits. With a monthly
rent of $950 and all the other expenses, it was not easy to get by. They had
about $1,750 a month to live on, having lost the government subsidies once
he got a job. In his free time, he often drove for Uber and Lyft to bring in
desperately needed cash.

Sadeqa spoke only a few words of English and only recently started taking English classes. Her days were spent taking care of the apartment and
being with friends in the same apartment complex who were from Afghanistan. Though Sadeqa was an Afghan university graduate, the language
barrier made it impossible to find work, and the isolation was especially
hard on her.

Although Jawad had served in the U.S. military, risked his life, and
helped the troops, he did not get any of the benefits that are provided to
veterans.

I applied for medical insurance and learned I had to pay almost $250
per month. We barely had enough money for shoes, clothes, for going
out to dinner with friends. If I paid $250 every month, the govern-
ment was also paying 70 percent of the insurance. If we got sick I'd
have to pay 30 percent more for doctors or medicine. We're trying to
not get sick, but it's life, we're human.

I wanted to return to school but I could not, because I had to make
sure that the bills were paid. I wanted to become an engineer, doing

work like I was doing back home, so I knew I had to go college and study hard. Otherwise I can't attain my dream. But if going to college means I have to cut my work hours, what should I do? Every day, every month, every year, I'm losing time. If I'm losing the time for the next couple of years, I will not be motivated for college. Now I am, but I have to work. I thank America for all the country has done for me, but helping people with education would mean they could accomplish more as citizens.

Jawad's dream is painfully distant. The path to citizenship will take five years for Jawad and Sadeqa.

It's so hard for me because I'm thinking if I'm going to die one day what happens to my family here, my wife? If I am going to get in an accident here, who will support me? Nobody. Being a refugee, it means you have nothing here, just you're on your own and you don't know the people. And you must work hard finding a solution. I am not familiar with any of the systems here. It is like I am starting life over.

Jawad is pained by the continued war in Afghanistan, ISIS (Islamic State of Iraq and Syria) moving in, the Taliban, and the heroin trade. He remains deeply proud of his Afghan roots but now sees a country lying in ruins and desperation. He so appreciates what the United States is trying to do but, like everyone, really does not know if the United States will succeed against so many other forces.

Jawad emphasizes that nearly all the refugees he knows are well educated and eager to contribute to America but are held back for many reasons: lack of fluency in English, lack of finances to attend school, no family support here in the United States, and discrimination.

Somehow Jawad and Sadeqa keep going. He is rooted in the values of Islam, what he learned from his family, and his own strength of identity. Even with all the challenges, he is extremely grateful to be in the United

States. He knows that one day it will work out. Jawad's story will continue to unfold in the years to come.

In 2018, Jawad was hired full time by World Relief in Sacramento as a cultural advisor helping other Afghan refugees adjust to life in America. Sadeqa's English has greatly improved. Both he and his wife are taking classes at American River College. Jawad is studying international relations.

Every day when I wake up, I tell myself, Okay Jawad, this is a new day, I must do something today, I must have a better day than yesterday. It's pushing me forward.

We have hope that one day Afghanistan will become a peaceful country. In the future, I would like to go back to visit. But for now it's not safe for me. For now, I have to become educated. It's like if you're going to go to a war zone, the bad guys are going to start shooting, and you can't be out of ammo. If you are, you have to go back to base to reload your weapons and then go back to war. Today I feel that I've shot all my ammunition in the war zone, so I'm back at base in the United States. Here I must reload myself, to educate myself and become something and get myself ready to do something of service for my people.

AFTERWORD

Over 2,000 years ago, the Greek philosopher Heraclitus offered this insight into the human condition: "Change is the only constant in life." That is certainly accurate when it comes to today's global refugee and migration crises. In the United States, the official government policy toward immigrants and refugees fluctuates almost on a daily basis. Comprehensive Immigration Reform seems to be long forgotten. There are new laws being written or strategies enforced and the public only becomes aware when there are major changes: President Trump ending the process of new applications for DACA (September 2017); the separation of families and children at our borders (June 2018); the Supreme Court upholding President Trump's travel ban against certain majority-Muslim countries (June 2018); and the president declaring a national emergency to acquire funds to build a wall along the border with Mexico (February 2019).

By the time this book goes to print, there will certainly be more changes, and without a profound reversal of policy, refugees or asylum seekers will be faced with a difficult, if even penetrable, process to be allowed to enter the United States. Life will be challenging for DACA beneficiaries and those eligible for the program. Despite their many contributions to our country—economically, in technology and science, socially, and culturally—they will be living on tenterhooks, unsure of their ability to stay in their new home.

The stories of the eleven people in this book will also continue to unfold—some for the better, some for the worse. The only thing that is certain is that their experiences up to this point illuminate their courage, perseverance, and belief in America as a land of freedom. Their stories contain indelible truths that help us understand the global suffering of millions of people who are simply looking to come to America to live safely, contribute in a meaningful way to our society, and enjoy the promise of basic human rights.

The United States is truly at a crossroads. Will Emma Lazarus's famous words inscribed on the Statue of Liberty, "Give me your tired, your poor, / Your huddled masses yearning to breathe free," become just a historic sentiment that has lost its meaning, or will it still shape America and its ethic of welcoming people to our shores and valuing all they can contribute?

What is needed now are discussions that go beyond politics and rhetoric to shape a comprehensive immigration reform policy that will be as fair as possible to American citizens, refugees, migrants, and everyone involved.

Now is the time for bold, creative thinking that realistically looks at the global migration issues of the twenty-first century as an American issue, one we must attack with vigor for the sake of freedom for all people who come to our doors.

ACKNOWLEDGMENTS

Gratitude does not capture what I feel toward everyone who has been part of this journey. The road that started for me in the Darfuri refugee camps of Chad in 2004 has been informed and inspired by so many people who provided me with the passion to write this book.

To the eleven remarkable men and women who have shared their stories with me for this book, I am deeply indebted. Their experiences as refugees have taught me much about life and its meaning. We have cried and laughed together. I thank them for their time, their willingness to talk about very difficult and sensitive events in their lives, and the many ways they enrich America.

The photo editor of the book and photographer of nine of the people, Dona Kopol Bonik, has captured the essence of each person with her gifted eye and skill. It has been a pleasure to work with her. I am also grateful to Jordan Scheiner, who was Asinja's photographer in Houston, and Michael A. Schwarz, who was Malk's photographer in Atlanta.

My conversations with Adam Mussa in the Kuonongo Refugee Camp in Chad and with Meron Semedar at the University of San Francisco played a key role in inspiring this work. Other refugees told their powerful stories in my classes as well. Among those are Leon Raninjer, Wilita Sanguma, Jean Pierre Ndagijimana, and Deng Jonkuch.

I am very thankful to those who reached out to connect me to the people featured in this book: Kirt Lewis, Mark Hetfield, Bill Swersey, Nancy Wilis, Daniel Ha, Bonnie Lowenthal, Norma Chinchilla, Kate Wadsworth, Zane Blechner, Gal Spinrad, Ali Al Sudani, and Karen Ferguson.

Cameron Gable and Jody Stella were excellent research assistants whose extensive work provided the background information for this book.

This book would not have come to fruition without the immeasurable guidance, support, and editing of Leslie Schnur, the editing of Adam Bell, and the work of my agent, Carol Mann, and her assistant Agnes Carlowicz. I am deeply grateful to Lisa Banning and Vincent Nordhaus, my editor and project manager from Rutgers University Press, as well as Brian Ostrander, production editor at Westchester Publishing Services, for guiding the process to publication.

Many people have given support and input in a variety of ways: Mark Hetfield, Jeff Salkin, Gary Zola, Michelle Lueck, Dave Eggers, Ingrid Gavshon, Aaron Hahn Tapper, Ben Bycel, Norman Fassler-Katz, and Jim Linden.

I am grateful to the International Medical Corps and its president, Nancy Aossey, for providing me with the opportunity to begin my work with refugees in many different countries. It was during my first trip with IMC that I met Adam Mussa, a Darfuri refugee, living in the Kounongo refugee camp in Eastern Chad.

My ability to do the research for this book was made possible by the generosity of Howard Unger and Caryn Stoll, David and Lisa Auerbach, Lisa Wade, Shirley Fredricks, Jay and Deanie Stein, Larry and Lauren Posner, and David and Lola Safer, as well as a dear friend who chooses to remain anonymous.

The classes I teach at the University of San Francisco and Congregation Beth Shalom of Napa Valley as well as the seminars I moderate at the Aspen Institute have provided me with many ideas and insights from students and fellow learners. The discussions about justice and goodness, human nature, and ways to improve the quality of life for all people have played a role in my birthing this book.

Researching, interviewing, and writing this book has been a labor of love and one that has consumed a lot of my time. My wife, Judy, has always been incredibly supportive, loving, and understanding, as have been my sons, Micah and Moti, and my daughters-in-law, Liat and Danielle. My beautiful grandchildren, Eva, Levi, Ayala, and Arlo, have provided me with the joy and pure love of life that has driven me to do this work. My hope is that they will see in their lifetimes a world that truly takes to heart the plight of refugees and develops policies that reflect compassion and a grandiosity of spirit that sees the humanity in each person.

INDEX

Wade, Lisa Frankel, 73–74
war, as cause for displacement, 5, 8.
  See also specific wars
Winfrey, Oprah, 47
World Relief, 104, 184, 185, 187
World War II, 155: American hostility
  toward German refugees during, 9;
  creation of the United Nations after,
  7; displaced people during, 8; and the
  Holocaust, 78–87; Italy in, and Italian
  East Africa, 16

xenophobia, 9, 10, 28, 42

Yazda, 60
Yazidis, 44–45, 46–48, 51, 52, 55, 60–61
youth: development, programs for,
  130–131, 155, 170; targeted in El
  Salvador for gang recruitment, 124.
  See also child slavery; child soldiers

Zahir Shah, 172
"Zero Tolerance" policy, 123

ABOUT THE AUTHOR

LEE BYCEL is a humanitarian activist, teacher, rabbi, and author who serves as the Sinton Visiting Professor of Holocaust, Ethics and Refugee Studies at the University of San Francisco. He has visited refugee camps in Darfur, Chad, South Sudan, Rwanda, Kenya, Ethiopia, and Haiti. He has written extensively about the plight of refugees, and has secured much-needed funding for medical clinics in refugee camps. Lee is known for his work as a senior moderator of seminars at the Aspen Institute, senior advisor for global strategy at the International Medical Corps, and the first executive director of the Redford Center. He has been a leader in the Jewish community for many years, serving for fifteen years as dean of the Hebrew Union College in Los Angeles. Lee served on the Board of the United States Holocaust Memorial Museum from 2014 until April 2019 and is a member of its Committee on Conscience. He is a past president of the Los Angeles County Commission on Human Relations.